The Magic of Writing

The Magic of Writing

How to Write and Publish the Book that is Inside You

Linda J Falkner

iUniverse, Inc.

New York Lincoln Shanghai

The Magic of Writing
How to Write and Publish the Book that is Inside You

iUniverse, Inc.

For information address:
iUniverse
2021 Pine Lake Road, Suite 100
Lincoln, NE 68512
www.iuniverse.com

ISBN: 0-595-29435-9

Printed in the United States of America

Contents

ACKNOWLEDGEMENTS

I want to thank all the people who encouraged me to write this book. There are more aspiring authors than I can name who expressed an interest in reading a book about how to write and publish. I especially want to thank David D'Aloia and Georgie Kovacs for their encouragement and support. I want to thank Ann Cook and Jane Shevtsov for their hard work proofreading and finding all the little mistakes that I warn my readers about. Mark Javer deserves recognition for his professional photography work in designing the cover for this book. You can enjoy more of his work at www.studiomgallery.com.

Many of the writing samples in this book came from my books *I Would Be Loved, Americans Lost,* and *Search for the Fountain: The Secret to Youthful Aging.* These books can be ordered through bookstores or over the Internet. For more information about me, and about my books, check my website www.FalknerBooks.com.

THE MAGIC OF WRITING:

How to write and publish the book that is inside you.

W hen I was in third grade, I had the ugliest, meanest witch of a teacher that ever lived. Mrs. Snaggletooth had worms on her head instead of hair, and a wart on the tip of her nose the size of a quarter with black hair growing out of it. She ate children for lunch. I hated her and refused to go to her class. All right, my parents made me take my body to her class every day, but they couldn't force me to be there mentally. I spent that year writing stories in my mind, and by the time I entered fourth grade, I knew that I would be a writer. It wasn't a "someday" thing; I was going to write a book when I was forty. I have no memory of how I chose that age, but that was the magical number that stuck in my mind.

I didn't know it at the time, but there is one huge difference between "someday" and "forty." You see, unlike someday, forty actually comes. When I hit my thirty-seventh birthday, I realized that I needed to get to work. The deadline was approaching quicker than I ever thought possible, and I hadn't the faintest idea how to write, much less how to get published, so I did two things—I joined the Tampa Writers Alliance and I began writing. My earliest work screamed "beginner." I made every mistake a writer could possibly make and a few extra that hadn't been invented. I was the expert on poor writing, but I learned. I completed my first book and had an agent accept it at the age of thirty-nine and eleven months, just a few weeks before my childhood goal arrived.

In the process of learning to write, I read a lot of how-to books, but *The Magic of Writing* is the book that I needed when I first began writing. This book will show you the mistakes that beginning writers make, and teach you how to write like a professional. It includes practice sessions to help you polish your work.

This book also discusses publishing. Once, not many years ago, there were only two choices. You could either get a royalty publisher, which was, and still remains unlikely, even if you have an agent, or you could put out big bucks to self-publish. People who self-publish have the problem of deciding what to do with a few thousand books sitting in their garage. Most self-published authors sell or give away a few hundred books, and moths eat the rest.

Modern printing now has allowed a new option called Print on Demand. With Print on Demand, everyone can get published, whether you have written a future best seller, or just a book about your life to share with your children and grandchildren. Initial set-up costs remain low with this new technology, and you may purchase as many books as you desire, or just one at a time.

Print on Demand lets you get your book listed with major on-line booksellers such as Amazon.com and Barnes and Nobles. This gives you the chance to sell your book worldwide without having to pay for printing and shipping costs. Most Print on Demand companies have no minimum requirements. All you need to do is to submit a completed manuscript, and pay their set-up costs, in order to put your work into a publishable format.

I'm not promising an easy path. This isn't a book you can pick up and read in a few days. This is a book you can use as a guide to help your writing become stronger, clearer, and help you communicate better. Even if you aren't interested in writing a book, you may wish to write a holiday greetings letter (or Christmas letter, if you aren't concerned with being politically correct), get a better grade on a term paper, or sell that important idea to Mr. Bigshot, who will be impressed with your clear, concise, and professional writing skills.

Chapter 1

HOW DO I BEGIN?

Have you ever had a job where you had to get up early in the morning, but some days you would have preferred to sleep late? So, what did you do? If you are like most of us, you groaned a bit, rubbed the sleep from your eyes, and staggered into the shower to wake up. The answer is, you went to work. Not only did you go to work one day, but you went day after day. You were there every day that you were scheduled to work, sometimes even when you had a terrible cold and felt half dead. You didn't talk about going to work "someday," or "when I have the time for it." No, you made the time for it, because keeping your job was important to you. Although I'm speaking in the past tense, I might as well say, "keeping your job IS important to you." Unless you are retired, your job isn't something that happened in the past and you finished—it's an ongoing, scheduled part of your life.

Now, with this in mind, there are a few things you need in order to begin making writing your job. You need a place to write, and unless you are a teenager, it probably isn't on your bed. My teenagers seem to have a talent for doing their homework in bed with the TV and radio blasting, but most adults need a quiet desk or writing space. I need a fairly clear area, but I've known other writers who do best in a clutter, surrounded by floor to ceiling books and papers, cigarettes, and a couple of big dogs. You know what you need to concentrate, so don't listen to anybody who tells you a better way.

You need to have a designated writing space or office. It doesn't matter if it's a special room just for writing, a desk in your bedroom, or a card table in a closet

1

that you share with the winter coats—your writing space is your office, and isn't used for anything else.

If you want to write, you need to make writing a high priority. You need to schedule writing on a regular basis, just as you do your job. You need to put writing time aside with the seriousness that you put aside your dinner hour or favorite television show. Until you have a set time when you are going to write, you might as well just dream about doing it someday. You will have plenty of company. These people are called "wannabes." Decide when you are going to write, and post these times on the door or a wall in your office. From now on you will refer to your writing as "work," and the place where you work as your "office."

ASSIGNMENT: Make yourself a sign with your office hours, the hours you will work (write). Even one hour a day will still make you a serious writer, but it's important to have a schedule and follow it.

Linda's Office Hours
Monday–Friday 7–9 am, 10–12 midnight
Saturday & Sunday 10am-12noon, 2–4pm

Here is my sign. I like to write before I go to my paying job in the morning, and before going to bed at night. I also try to use the weekends to accomplish a full day of writing. Usually I can only write for two hours and then my mind starts wandering, so I never schedule more time than that. However, I'm not limited to only writing during office hours. If I'm hot on an idea, I may write for many more hours. This is only a minimum daily writing schedule. Also, it's okay to cheat occasionally and take a day off, but try not to take off two days in a row because you'll lose your momentum and this can lead to writer's block. Now hang your sign in your office. It is especially important that you take yourself seriously enough to believe that you have an office with working hours. If your friends and family think you are losing your mind, ignore them.

WRITING WITH STYLE

Beginning writers worry about style. When I was just starting out, I began a story that was so bad that the Tampa Writers Alliance nearly laughed me out of the meeting. I thought I had developed my own style, but I had merely filled a page with every beginner's mistake possible. Developing a writer's style without developing basic writing skills might be compared to developing your own style of singing by singing whatever notes come into your mind, rather than those written for the song. I've been known to do this, and I'm afraid I don't get many encores. It takes hard work to learn to sing the correct notes, but until you do that, you aren't ready to develop your own style. Once you learn the notes to a song, or the skills for writing well, your style will become as unique and natural as you are. Don't worry about style, concentrate on learning to write well and style will take care of itself.

WRITING TOOLS

As in any craft, having the correct tools for writing is essential. The tools you need to begin are: a comfortable ink pen in a pleasing color, a small notepad that fits in your pocket or purse, a larger notepad, and a computer with a good word processing program.

Although people have written for thousands of years without computers, you will find it invaluable for writing well. If you don't have, or can't afford a computer, you can purchase a word processing machine for very little money. However, the computer has one huge advantage over a word processor because the Internet is invaluable for research.

ASSIGNMENT: Get a notebook or writing pad with lined paper (college or wide rule, whatever you are most comfortable with), and a pen (or pencil if you prefer). The pen does not have to be expensive, but it should be comfortable to hold, a color you like (as you will be seeing a lot of it in the next few weeks), and has ink that flows smoothly without leaking or leaving blobs.

GETTING STARTED

Where is your favorite place to go out to eat? I want you to think about writing as an enjoyable activity, so get your notebook and special writing pen and go out to dinner—alone. Writing is not a social activity, so get used to doing your work alone. However, if you find a friend who also wants to write, and the two of you decide to write as a team, then bring your friend. Don't bring any young children. You might want to choose a fast food restaurant, that place where the service seems to take years, or a food-court in a mall. You might prefer another place where people gather. A football game, flea market, bingo game, or airport, are other excellent choices.

While you are sitting at the table, look around. Spend some time watching and listening to people. When you find somebody who looks interesting, begin writing about him or her, and describing what that person looks like—the girl looks about sixteen years old. She has bleached blond hair with red and blue streaks. She is wearing white make-up with black lipstick. She is wearing a blue T-shirt with the word, "Superdog."

After you have gotten comfortable describing how people look, you will want to describe what they are doing: The girl is holding hands with a young man about her age. He has spiked green hair and his pants are falling down. They are talking to each other. Now they are kissing and whispering in each other's ear.

After you have practiced describing what people look like, and what they are doing, you will want to start writing down what they are saying. "Oh, Bobby, I can't marry you because I've enrolled in the Army and will be leaving next week," she said.

At this point, it doesn't have to be good, and you probably won't want to share it with anybody. The idea is to start writing, and real live people, ordinary people doing ordinary things, are your best subjects.

ASSIGNMENT: Spend at least an hour every day observing people. Look at what they are wearing, how they are acting, and what they are saying. Observe people while at work, in the grocery store, while buying gas, and waiting in line. Write at least one paragraph each day describing how someone looks, and what they are doing or saying. Keep a small notepad with you at all times and jot down notes when you observe interesting people or overhear conversations.

KEEP THE MOMENTUM GOING

Most writers I've known seem to have an addiction to collecting and reading books. Reading is an excellent way to prepare for writing. I often spend several weeks, or even months, reading about a new topic before I tackle it on paper. Like most writers, I write about things that I enjoy reading, and thus I am both interested in and knowledgeable about my subject. I don't care to read love stories, so it's unlikely that I will ever write one. If you hate mysteries, but the love of your life thinks you should write a mystery novel, nod and smile, but write what interests YOU.

If you are serious about writing, it's important to write everyday. You already have set office hours, and in addition to this, you want to set a minimum number of pages that you will complete each day. One page a day is an adequate number to get started with. Does that sound too easy? It's okay to do more, but you need to set a goal that won't be too difficult to accomplish. If you set a goal of ten pages per day, you will end up quitting in frustration. One page a day adds up to one hundred and sixty-two pages in six months. Yes, by writing just one page every day, you can write a short, but respectable book in half a year. However, you can expect to take more time, as most of writing is rewriting, and rewriting, and rewriting again. The words you put on paper are never sacred, and can always be improved.

But what if you are someone who worries about writer's block? As far as I can tell, there's no such thing as writer's block. What there is, is "sitter's block." You need to sit your behind on a chair, turn on the computer, or open your notebook, and begin writing. You can't overcome writer's block by thinking about your story while going for a walk, caring for the kids, watching TV, reading e-mail, playing computer games, or surfing the net. You can only overcome writer's block if you are writing.

"But I can't think of anything to write," you may say. "Worrying about writing ten pages a day isn't my problem. I find one page overwhelming."

That's okay; here are some ideas to get started. Take your notes and write about the people you have been observing (you have been observing, right? If not and you are stuck, go back and do this). Imagine what that old woman pushing her husband in a wheelchair is going to do when she gets home from the mall. You were concerned about that pregnant teenager? Imagine what her life is going to be like caring for a baby. That young boy with a baseball T-shirt caught your eye? Write about his game next week.

The newspaper is another wonderful place to get ideas. Take the beginning of a story from the paper, and then let your imagination flow. The characters will develop a life of their own and you will be surprised what comes from your fingers.

Still have no imagination, just can't manage to write anything about the people you saw? That's okay, write about what you ate for breakfast, or describe how to cook your favorite dinner. Write a shopping list, write a letter to your friend, write your epitaph. Write.

Another good way to get started is to copy a page from a book by your favorite author. Copying other people's work will help you develop a flow, and give you the chance to write until you feel comfortable writing your own words. As long as you don't try selling it as your work, it's perfectly okay to write a book that's already been written by someone else.

ASSIGNMENT: Practice writing until you have a short story. It doesn't have to be good, and it doesn't have to be long. A few pages are fine. Now that you are a writer (if you write, then you are a writer), it's time to begin polishing your work.

RESEARCH

Don't panic over the word "research." It isn't too difficult. By research, I mean the times when you have a question regarding something important to your story, and will want to use the Internet or other sources to look up facts. You may even want to write someone who is an expert in the field and ask for information. The Internet brings the world to you at a touch. Even fiction books need accurate information. You don't want your characters in 1801 driving along a superhighway. If your facts are incorrect, you will lose credibility with your readers.

All genres, including science fiction, require accurate facts to be believable. If you have cockroaches suddenly develop on a sterile planet, or a medically impossible disease occurs, your readers won't believe you. When the impossible occurs, you need a good explanation based on either real facts, or in science fiction, consistent invented facts (warp drive, for example).

Historical novels are often based on extensive research, but so are mysteries, or any other genre which describes a certain town or real place. Even if the place is invented, it must have enough accurate facts to seem real.

IMPORTANT WARNING

There is a name for people who talk about their stories before they write them. They are called "wannabe writers". To prevent yourself from becoming a wannabe writer, once you have a story in your mind, DO NOT talk about the story. Don't tell anybody. If your spouse, mother, or best-friend-in-the-world asks you about the story—DON'T talk about it. Don't talk about it to your hair cutter. Don't even talk about it to your psychiatrist. Tell them you have a great idea for a story, and they can be the first to read it. If you talk about the story, you won't have the same driving need to write it. Once you let the story out, it's gone forever. Don't let it out through your mouth. The correct way to let a story out is through your fingers. Type or write it, but don't ever talk it away.

"The difference between the right word and the almost right
word is the difference between lightning and the lightning bug."

Mark Twain

Chapter 2

CORRECTING COMMON MISTAKES.

If you wish to get the greatest benefit out of this book, it's important that you have at least a few pages of your own writing that you'd like to polish. I hope you will consider this a workbook for improving your work. Of course, feel free to keep on reading just for pleasure and information. However, if you don't have any of your own writing yet, I suggest you return to chapter one and follow the suggestions about writing. I know you are an intelligent person and don't need me to spoon-feed you with my writing samples, so although I will be giving a few examples, I'm leaving it up to you to supply most of the writing. I expect that you are more interested in polishing your own masterpiece than doing assignments I have invented for you, anyway. It doesn't matter if you have written a short story, a longer work, a paper for a class, or even a job assignment, and it doesn't matter how good, or bad, your writing is, as long as you have work that you want help polishing.

Do you know how to use the word find on your computer? If you do, you may skip to the next section. If not, these directions are for Microsoft Word. Look to the top left of the page. There are several words: File, Edit, View, etc. Go to the second word, "edit," and click on it with your mouse. The second to last word on the pull-down list says, "find" and has a binoculars icon. Click on find. When I ask you to find a word such as "do" or "was," type that word into the box. Then click the middle box in the bottom right that says, "Find next." This will bring you to the word that you are searching for. Continue this process until you have found every occurrence of the word in question. If you have another program, and don't know how to locate word find, don't ask me—ask a teenager.

DO, DID

Good writing is clear and concise, without extra words. The words do and did are words that are often abused. Here are some examples of how to remove these words to improve your writing.

Change "She **did walk** to the store" to "She **walked** to the store."

I do like ice cream.	I like ice cream.
He did run a race.	He ran a race.
Sue did show up for her appointment.	Sue showed up for her apartment.
Frank did eat all the pie.	Frank ate all the pie.
They did jump rope.	They jumped rope.

ASSIGNMENT 1: Go through your story using the word find function on your computer. If you don't have a computer, read your story aloud to find "do" and "did." Remove all these words, and fix your sentences. In some contexts "do" is necessary. Examples might be: We do that every day. What do you do at work? How do you want your meat cooked?

ASSIGMENT 2: Make up a 3x5 card with the following title "Words to Avoid." If you found you used the words "do" or "did," then add those words to your card. You will want to refer to this card often when you first start writing.

BY

The word "by" indicates a passive sentence. Passive sentences are wordy and confusing. They frustrate and bore the reader. Passive sentences indicate lazy writing. Always take the time to write well. Take the time and effort to find and correct your passive sentences. Here are some examples of passive and active sentences:

Passive	Active
The wagon was pushed by the boy.	The boy pushed the wagon
It was paid for by the man.	The man paid for it.

She was hit by Billy.   Billy hit her.
This book was written by Linda Falkner.   Linda Falkner wrote this book.

ASSIGNMENT: Use your word find to locate the word "by" and change all passive sentences to active sentences. Your computer may be set to underline passive sentences. If it isn't, and you don't know how to change the settings, ask a teenager. If this was a problem area for you, add the word "by" to your 3x5 card. Of course, there are times when the word "by," is fine to use because it doesn't form a passive sentence. "He walked by my house," is an example.

WAS

You'll notice that the word "was" is part of a passive sentence. When you changed your sentences from passive to active, you not only took out the word "by" but also the word "was."

However, "was" and "were" are usually found in sentences without the word "by." "Was" is an excellent word to look for in your word find. It tells you that your sentence needs to be examined to see if you can improve your writing. When you remove "was," you may want to look at the sentence to see if you can add more details. Here are some examples.

Weak sentences   Better

The dog was wagging its tail.   The dog wagged its tail.
The girl was going to the store.   The girl went to the store.
The boy was throwing a ball.   The boy threw a ball.
The dog was barking.   The dog barked.

Now, lets add more detail to the sentence "The dog was happy." The first detail that is missing is the kind of dog. Was this a big dog, a small dog, a brown spotted dog? Lets change this sentence to "The chihuahua was happy." While this is better, I still see the word "was," and this indicates to me that this sentence needs more work. My next question is, "how do you know that the dog was happy?" Answering this question clarifies this sentence and removes the offending "was." The sentence can now be made to read, "The chihuahua wagged its tail." Now you don't need to tell the reader that the chihuahua was happy, because you showed it with an action.

Let's try another one. "The girl was depressed." I have two questions: "what girl?" and "how do you know?" I would rewrite this sentence to read:

Mary shuffled into the doctor's office. Her eyes were red from crying and the receptionist overheard her telling another patient in the waiting room that she wanted to kill herself.

Now, I have answered both questions. The girl was Mary, and you know she was depressed because I showed you how she acted, rather than told you she was depressed. Let the reader figure this out for himself through the action.

"They were playing." How about rewriting this to read: Bob and Joe played baseball.

Another advantage to removing the "was" or "were" is that it opens your sentence to write more detail. "They were playing" stops me dead. I have nothing more to say. However, "Bob and Joe played baseball," has the potential for a story. Where did they play? Who won? What were the details of the game? As I write this, there is a rainstorm, and I've decided to incorporate this into the sentence:

Bob and Joe played baseball all afternoon in the rain.

ASSIGNMENT: Go through your word find to locate "was" and "were." Rewrite your sentence to remove these words. Add details to show what happened. Don't tell the reader your story—*show it*. Add the words "was" and "were" to your "Words To Avoid" card.

ING

You may have noticed that when you removed "was" or "were," you also removed "ing" from the verb. "Susan was walking" changed to "Susan walked." "Mark was throwing the ball," is crisper and clearer when written, "Mark threw the ball." Removing "ing" from action words helps keep your writing simple, crisp, and clear. Here are a few more examples.

Poor	Better
The dog was wagging its tail.	The dog wagged its tail.
The children were laughing.	The children laughed.
Mary was jumping on the bed.	Mary jumped on the bed.
The cat was climbing the tree.	The cat climbed the tree.

ASSIGNMENT: Search for "ing" endings and change them to a past tense when appropriate.

Of

"Of" is another great word for identifying weak sentences. Unless you are talking about a proper name, such as Cream-of-Wheat, this is a good word to find and remove. Here are a few examples.

Weak	Better
I prefer chocolate instead of vanilla.	I prefer chocolate. I don't care for vanilla.
Because of her, I lost my glasses.	I lost my glasses when the sexy woman distracted me.
I thought of my house.	I thought about my house.
A can of soup	canned soup
A glass of milk	milk

Often, you can't remove the word "of" without rewriting the sentence, but doing so strengthens the story. The following story uses the word "of" four times, and the word "was" twice. I'm not going to try to rewrite it, rather, I am going to throw the sentence away and start over using the same idea. You'll see that without this baggage, I'm able to give much more detail, and write a better story.

Going to college **was** always a dream **of** mine, but because **of** my dad, I never went. It **was** because **of** his father that he never went. I accepted it, **of** course.

My grandfather couldn't afford to send my father to college. Gramps felt embarrassed about being poor, and didn't want to admit his poverty to his son. Instead, he told pops that a college education wastes good money and time. Pops could have afforded to send me to college, but he continued hearing his father's messages about college and discouraged me. I accepted my fate with resignation.

ASSIGNMENT: Use word find to search for the word "of." Rewrite each sentence, deleting this word. Add "of" to your "Words To Avoid" card if this is a problem word for you.

-ly Adverbs

When I was a student in school, I saw no use for naming nouns, verbs, adverbs, and all the rest. I knew how to talk even if I didn't know the name of parts of speech. Maybe you were the rare student who pleased your teacher and learned to name each speech part. Either way, being able to label parts of speech doesn't make you a good writer. However, knowing how to use these named, or unnamed, parts of speech *is* essential to good writing. There are a group of words that end in the letters "ly". These are called adverbs and include happily, gladly, sadly, beautifully, and adjectives such as lovely. You were probably taught to use them when you were in grade school, but they weaken your writing. These are easy to deal with—find them on the computer and delete them. Here are some examples of -ly word sentences:

Weak sentences	Better
The girl happily joined him in a dance.	The girl joined him in a dance.
The dog barked loudly.	The dog howled.
The woman spoke loudly	The woman yelled.
The boy quickly ran through the bushes.	The boy sprinted through the bushes.
The girl quietly walked across the room.	The girl tiptoed across the room.

English has many expressive verbs like tiptoed, sprinted, yelled, and howled. Rather than using an "ly" adverb with a weak verb, use the strongest verb, or action word, that you can find.

When I was a beginning writer, writing a book length manuscript seemed overwhelming. I decided that I would develop a new "style". This "style" consisted of adding as many "ly" words to my story as I could possibly fit in. The results would have been comical if I hadn't been so pleased with my work. I was depending on "ly" words to supply details and length to my story. I lacked the knowledge of how to show, rather than tell. Here is an example of a story with "ly" words.

The girl happily crossed the stream and watched the white horse sleep peacefully. She quickly got her saddle and caught the horse. She rode the horse giddily and laughed loudly.

The problem here is that the author is using "ly" words to tell the story, rather than strong verbs to show the actions. Here is a rewrite, doing nothing more than removing the offending adverbs.

The girl crossed the stream and watched the white horse sleep. She got her saddle and caught the horse. She rode the horse and laughed.

This last paragraph isn't meant to demonstrate great writing, but it shows the improvement that occurs in a sentence when "ly" adverbs are removed. The reader doesn't want or need the author to spoon-feed him with adverbs.

ASSIGNMENT: Set the word find to ly. Skip one space following the "ly" so the computer doesn't stop in the middle of words. Remove each "ly" word, and if possible, find a stronger verb to express what you were trying to say with your "ly".

EXCLAIMATION MARKS!!!!!!!!!!!!!!!!!!!!!!!!

Exclamation marks are a way of telling the reader that this is where you need to add excitement. It's a bit like having a laugh track on television. If the story is written well, people will know when to laugh, or when to be excited. If it isn't written well, then the exclamation mark isn't going to fix the problem.

ITALICS

Italics are like exclamation marks in that they tell the reader where emphasis needs to be. It's much better to show this to the reader through careful writing.

ASSIGNMENT: Check your work for exclamation marks and italics. Rewrite the sentence so you show the excitement or emphasis without these unnecessary and distracting methods. Use them sparingly, if at all.

AVOID VAGUE, OVERUSED WORDS

Words such as "nice," "awful," "wonderful," "very," "so," and "quite" can be included in your list of weak words. A sentence such as "It was a very nice house" doesn't give any description and doesn't do anything to make the reader want to continue reading. A quaint cottage, a huge castle, are other examples of boring non-descriptions. Instead of using overworked words, describe what the house looked like.

Her immaculate apartment in an upper-middle-class neighborhood was filled with African designs, artificial plants, wooden statues, and a variety of both wooden and stuffed animals, including a life-sized stuffed tiger. I had the feeling I had walked into an African museum display.
"I enjoy collecting," Wertha said.

You notice here how I described the apartment with specific descriptions. The reader could walk into her apartment after reading this paragraph and recognize that this is Wertha's home, and nobody else's. I don't tell you the apartment is nice, attractive, or unique, as you can figure this out for yourself.

REPEATING WORDS

It's easy to get one word in your mind and use it repeatedly in a story or paragraph without realizing that you have done so. Even experienced writers have to watch for this. It may be a word like "very," or "that," or possibly "enormous." You won't be aware that you are overusing a word while you are writing, so, while proofreading, you need to look for redundant words. Here are some examples. See if you can find and correct the repeated words:

I thought that you were going to the grocery store, but instead of that, you went to the hardware store. That was a good idea because that store is where you can buy that shovel you need.

"Store" was used three times, "that" was used five times, and "you" was used four times. "Of" was used once, but should be removed. Here is an improved version. Notice I changed hardware store to Home Depot, which gives more information regarding which hardware store the person went to.

I thought you were going to the grocery store, but instead, you went to Home Depot. That was a good idea because they carry shovels.

Here is another example:

This is a story about an enormous two-headed dog. In this story, the man walked carefully into an enormous

cave and saw this enormous two-headed dog. The man
was quite frightened and wanted to run away, but the cave
was so enormous that the man hid instead, and the
enormous two-headed dog never noticed the man.

This story has more filler than context. Repeating words fills up space on the page, but weakens your writing. Here is my rewrite of the above story.

Robert crept into the cave where the two-headed dog lived.
The dog was the size of a Boeing 747 and Robert shuddered as
he watched saliva rain from the dogs drooling jowls.
He found a rock and climbed under it before the monster noticed him.

Here is one more example:

When Fred won the lottery, he was very, very, happy. He jumped up and
down until he was very out of breath. He was so very happy.

The word "very" was used four times and "happy" was used twice. It's almost like the child who was asked to write a page in school and wrote: I am very, very, very, very, very, very, very, happy. "Very happy" is a poor choice of words for someone who had just won the lottery. A stronger word like "ecstatic" or "elated," would show how Fred was feeling. The word "so" also needs to be removed. Here is the sentence rewritten:

When Fred won the lottery, he was ecstatic. He ran in circles and jumped
up and down until he couldn't catch his breath.

This sentence would be even better if we leave out the first sentence, which tells how Fred feels, and just show how Fred feels:

When Fred won the lottery, he ran in circles and jumped
up and down until he couldn't catch his breath.

This is an example of the writing, and rewriting process. Each time I read a sentence, I find a way to improve it. However, this sentence still has a problem. "Catch his breath" is a cliché. I need to find a fresh and original way to express this thought.

IDIOMS AND CLICHÉS

Clichés are common everyday expressions that we all use without realizing it, but they can mean different things to different people. Beginning writers often support weak writing with cleaver, but overused expressions. It is better to explain what you mean in your own original way.

Idioms are expressions unique to a language. They are sure to stump foreign language speakers just learning English. An idiom such as "I missed the boat" has nothing to do with a boat, and couldn't be understood if you weren't familiar with the idiom. A well-written story doesn't need idioms or clichés—and is stronger without them. The only exception is dialog, where a character may use clichés or idioms in his speech. If you take the extra effort to find and remove overused expressions, you will clarify and improve your writing.

Idioms	Better choice
Ann baked the cake **from scratch.**	Ann used a recipe to bake the cake.
My aunt is **nutty as a fruitcake**.	Aunt Dorothy ran outside naked.
Fred was **on top of the world**.	Fred couldn't sleep for three days after winning. the lottery

Clichés	
I am free as a bird	I could go anywhere I chose.
He lives a charmed life	He is lucky and good things happen to him.
Christmas comes but once a year	You can't expect gifts (great things) everyday.
He was frightened out of his wits	He was so frightened he ran a mile without stopping.

I took the first list from a book listing idioms, and the second from a computer list of clichés. Don't worry if idioms and clichés seem similar to you, because you shouldn't be using either. Take the time to find and rewrite idioms, clichés, and overused expressions using your own, fresh language. Clichés and idioms are neither creative nor original, and are a result of lazy writing.

ASSIGNMENT: Get a book on clichés/idioms from a bookstore or library. You don't need to memorize it (most likely an impossible feat), but spend some time looking through it to familiarize yourself with common expressions. Listen to people talk and pay attention to their expressions. Listen to yourself and try to discover what idioms and clichés you use. Check your writing and change overused expressions into sentences that show the action. You won't be able to use the word find function to locate idioms and clichés unless you use the same expression often. Reading aloud will help you find the unwanted idioms in your story. Also look for overused and repeated words. If you can't find any, ask a friend to read it and help you find them, or put your paper away for at least a week, and then come back and try again. It's easier to find mistakes once your work has rested for a while.

Chapter 3

SHOWING YOUR STORY

USE ACTION, NOT FEELING

Imagine you are watching a movie:

> The bad guy walks into the tavern and he is mad, furious, pissed, and ready to kill. The good guy looks up and grabs his gun...

How did you know what the bad guy felt? Do you suppose he walked into the tavern and said "Hey Joe, I'm really, really mad, in fact, I'm enraged with you. I'm going to kill you." Of course not. You knew because:

> Evil Sam walked into the bar glaring at Joe Good.
> He twisted his black mustache as he stood with his legs
> spread. Then Evil Sam spit, and as the saliva flew into
> the air, he grabbed his gun and aimed it at Joe Good, but
> Joe's gun was already cocked and pointing at Sam's forehead.

Notice that at no time did the story tell you how Evil Sam felt. It showed you with actions. This type of writing is easier to do if you imagine you are watching a movie. There is no need for a background voice saying: Sam is mad. And Sam won't say it either, but yet, you know from the actions. Movies are easy to show rather than tell, so always imagine that your book is a scene from a movie. Avoid words which tell how a character feels, and show it instead.

Telling words—Avoid using them.	Showing words—Use these instead
happy	laugh, smile, jump up and down
sad	cry, whine, whimper, sniffle
angry	glare, yell, scream, punch, throw
tired	sleep, eyes closing, yawn
exasperated	hit the table, stamped her feet
shy	hid behind her mother's skirt, last in line, doesn't talk
outgoing	pushed to the front, spoke first, grabbed the biggest...
excited	jumped, yelled, laughed, ran in circles
frightened	hid in the corner, said nothing, stared

WARNING: Be careful not to include telling words when using showing words. Examples of this are: She jumped for joy; he laughed with happiness; they cried with agony. Telling takes away from showing and weakens your writing.

Learning to show rather than tell a story is important in all kinds of writing. Showing, rather than telling, can even improve a term paper or technical writing. I'm going to save technical writing for another chapter and concentrate on fictional writing here, but I want to emphasis that showing is an essential part of all good writing, both fiction and nonfiction. Learning to show in your writing is an invaluable skill, but it takes practice to master.

Lets work on a story together. This first version tells what happens, but fails to show any action. It's sketchy and needs work. It includes many basic writing mistakes discussed in chapter two.

Susan was quite happy about her new pet. She was playing happily with her dog until the dog bit her. Susan was very upset after that.

Here is the improved version, taking out unnecessary words and showing rather than telling.

Susan's parents gave her a brown terrier-mix puppy for her birthday. She ran with the puppy and forgot about her other presents. She played chase and catch with the puppy for several hours and when the puppy attempted to sleep, she nudged it to wake it up. When the exhausted puppy nipped at Susan's nose, she ran to her mother crying.

SHOWING: Notice how much detail I added. When I removed words that told how Susan feels, I let my audience fill in the gaps, and made my readers an active part of the story. Although I removed the words "was," "quite," "happy," "playing," "happily" and "upset," the final version is longer and contains more detail.

Now, let's go through this story and break down what I did to change it from telling to showing. The first sentence "Susan was quite happy about her new pet," has numerous flaws. Quite is used as a filler, and adds nothing to the sentence. "Happy" tells Susan's feelings, but doesn't show us anything. Lastly, "pet" is vague and gives little information. As far we know, the new pet might have been a bird, a cat, a spider, or even a spiny anteater. This sentence doesn't give any information about where Susan got this pet, or why. When you write a sentence like this, you are feeding the reader baby food—bland and mushy. You haven't given the reader any reason to continue reading your story, and you have committed what I consider one of the greatest crimes of writing, you bored the reader. Here is the sentence again:

Susan was quite happy about her new pet.

Here is the first sentence rewritten into two sentences to answer the above questions:

Susan's parents gave her a brown terrier-mix puppy for her birthday. She ran with the puppy and forgot about her other presents.

Here is the next sentence:

She was playing happily with her dog until the dog bit her.

This leaves me with several questions. How does one play happily? If I told a hundred actors to "play happily," I think I'd see a hundred different versions of this action. You need to change this to show how Susan played. Now I'm left with a second question, and that is to ask why the dog bit her. It seems as though there is some missing information. I don't know if Susan abused the puppy, if she accidentally stepped on it, or if it was a vicious dog. The next sentence was rewritten to answer these questions:

She played chase and catch with the puppy for several hours and when the puppy attempted to sleep, she nudged it to wake it up.

This next sentence: "…the dog bit her." leaves more questions. Where was the bite, and how serious was it?

The rewritten sentence, the exhausted puppy nipped at Susan's nose, answers these questions.

Now here is the last sentence:

Susan was very upset after that.

My question is, "how does the reader know that Susan was upset?"
And the answer is, "she ran to her mother crying."
Here are some sentences for you to change from telling to showing. There is no one right answer, and everyone will interpret these statements differently. Try this:

The dog was happy.

The two questions you need to ask are what dog, and how did it show that it was happy. Here are some possible answers. In each case, notice I removed the word "was" along with the telling word "happy."

Rover wagged his tail.
The Great Dane knocked over the little girl and licked her face.
The German Shepard ran around in circles.
The Chihuahua, Jose, fell asleep on Michael's lap.

Here are some other sentences. Change them from telling to showing. Pretend you are directing a movie script, and you must tell the actor what to do. If the actions are performed well, it won't be necessary to tell the audience what the actor is feeling. Be sure you don't leave inexact descriptions such as "the girl" or "the cat." Your movie, like your story, needs each character described with at least some detail. Minor characters won't need as much description as major characters, but don't forget to give the audience at least a sketch.

The girl was depressed. (First you need to know what girl, does she have a name, and how do you know she was depressed. Be careful not to use telling words such as she cried with sadness. Crying shows an action, but sadness tells, and this weakens the sentence).

The boy was happy. (A boy being happy isn't going to look the same as it did for a dog).

The cat was angry.

Her mother is angry.

The boys were angry.

Susan is tired. (Beware the cliché "couldn't keep her eyes open").

He is outgoing.

They are mischievous.

Here are my answers. Yours will be different, but they should show action and avoid telling. Give specific details rather than feelings.

I changed: The girl was depressed to:

Mary lay in bed all day, crying.

The boy was happy

Rodger jumped around the room cheering when his father bought him a baseball glove for his birthday.

The cat was angry.

The black cat hissed at the dog.

Her mother is angry.

Jody's mother froze when she found the broken antique vase.

The boys were angry.

Bob and Andrew faced each other with fists raised in the air.

Susan is tired.

Susan never made it into her bed and fell asleep on the floor.

He is outgoing.

Aaron runs to the door when company arrives.

They are mischievous.

Tom and Matthew dug a hole in the ground and covered it with a light cloth and leaves.

ASSIGNMENT: Read through your work and look for examples where you are telling the story. Change them to showing. Imagine you are watching a movie, and ask yourself, "What would that *look like?*" Don't get discouraged if your whole story is telling and you have to rewrite large parts over. If you are finding mistakes that you missed when you wrote this story, then give yourself a big pat on your back for doing a good job. Most of writing is rewriting, not just once, but many times.

"I find television very educating. Every time somebody turns on the set, I go into the other room and read a book."

Groucho Marx

Chapter 4

PUTTING IT ALL TOGETHER

TRANSITIONS

Recently, I observed a high school class writing a paragraph. The teacher was showing them how to begin with a topic sentence and to write transitions; to connect each sentence to the next one, and to the topic. The goal was not to teach the students good writing, or to inspire children to enjoy writing, but to pass the Florida Comprehensive Achievement Test. Here is the outcome:

HOW TO BUY A GOOD GIFT
There are many qualities of a good gift. One quality is that
the gift is something that a person needs.
Clothing is a good gift because everyone needs to stay warm.
Therefore, people can give jackets and sweaters for Christmas.

Let's stop here and examine what this teacher was showing the students. They began with a topic sentence, talking about the qualities of a good gift. The first sentence mentioned qualities of a good gift. The second sentence tied into this using the word "quality" again, and expanded on it, describing a gift as something a person needs. The third sentence built on the need, mentioning that everybody needs to stay warm. The final sentence used the word "therefore" as a transition to the final thought that sweaters and jackets make good gifts.

This story is flat because it lacks details. It tells but doesn't show. The word "good" doesn't inspire much interest in this story, and a stronger topic, such as "An awesome gift," would add interest to the story. The repeated use of "that" in "One quality is **that** the gift is something **that** a person needs," is an example of poor word choice. However, the goal of the assignment wasn't to write an interesting story but to show the students how to form transitions between sentences and paragraphs. The story continued with this same idea. The second paragraph, still flat and lacking details or interest, did a good job of connecting the sentences together and transitioning from the first the paragraph into the second.

> While clothing is a good gift, people also need entertainment.
> Specifically, a television is a great gift for entertainment. A
> television is a great gift for any occasion.

In further paragraphs, the teacher encouraged the students to use words such as "therefore," "however," "specifically," "for example," and "in conclusion."

While these transitional words can be helpful if not overused, another technique for forming smooth transitions is to repeat words, and to overlap ideas from one sentence to the next. Transitions must not be obvious, but there needs to be a connection from one sentence to the next, and from one paragraph to the next. Each sentence should appear to flow effortlessly into the next. Each paragraph is a single idea, and each paragraph needs to blend smoothly into the next one. Your reader should never have to backtrack or try to figure out how you got from the previous point to the present one.

Here is a writing sample from my book *I Would Be Loved*. Look for the transitions between sentences and paragraphs. Watch how each paragraph connects to the next one by repeating the same idea, in this case the word "wish." I began talking about Christmas, which led naturally into Rosey's wish. The second paragraph was Rosey talking about her wish, and the final paragraph introduced the caseworker, but still continued with the main subject, "the wish."

> November turned into December and Christmas was everywhere—trees, Santa Claus, the first flurries of snow. While other children were thinking of Santa Claus and presents, Rosey had a special wish.
>
> "Rosey go home Christmas. Rosey see Mommy, Daddy, Joey, Baby. Rosey live home."
>
> The caseworker knew about Rosey's wish.

Many beginning writers put multiple ideas into one paragraph. They might write the equivalent of: The dog was happy. The cat ran away. The bird flew off.

They believe they are writing a paragraph because all the sentences relate to animals. This is too broad, and the sentences lack detail. In the last chapter, you learned to change sentences than tell into sentences that show. The three sentences above need to be changed into three separate paragraphs, and each one needs to include showing. Try rewriting them. Your results will differ from mine, but should be rich in detail, and each sentence needs to connect to the previous one. In the same way, each paragraph must blend smoothly from one idea into the next.

Here is one possible story using the dog, cat, and bird. Notice that each animal is given the time and attention that it needs, and each gets a full paragraph of its own. The story transitions smoothly from one animal to the other by overlapping:

The German shepherd woke from a deep sleep as the cat walked past him. He shook his head and stretched before sniffing the air. The cat smell that had wakened him hung in the air, and he breathed in again, trying to locate the feline. He wagged his tail and allowed his tongue to loll from his mouth. He sniffed the air again, and there was no question in his mind. He smelled cat.

The tiger striped stray watched the dog from atop a wooden fence. She knew there was food in his dog bowl, but she couldn't find a way to reach it without risking contact with the dog. While the hunger pangs continued, she watched a bird fly and then settle under a bush.

The blue jay flew under the bush to escape the noonday sun. She settled motionless, and didn't see the cat stalking her until it was too late. Sensing something wrong, she opened her wings in an attempt to fly at the same instant the hungry cat sprang. The couple met in midair, and the bird's demise meant another days survival for the stray cat.

Here are three more paragraphs from my book *Americans Lost* that demonstrate paragraphs flowing smoothly from one idea into another. Notice how each idea slightly overlaps into the next. This results in smooth transitions and an easily followed story:

"In thirteen years of being a bureaucrat, working with a multitude of families, this program, Homeless Recovery, has not moved one person from the street to self-sufficiency, which is our stated goal. We receive millions of dollars but have not moved one person out of homelessness, and I think I deserve bureaucrat of the year for that." James laughs.

"They get out of it themselves!" I exclaim.

"Exactly. Sixty to sixty-six percent of our families have gotten themselves self-sufficient. By this, we mean that they are totally on their own for three to six months, and have overcome a difficulty that would have previously put them on the street."

TIGHT WRITING

Be careful to keep your work tight. Make sure that each word, and each sentence, fits into the paragraph. Don't be unnecessarily wordy. It's easy to add additional ideas that, no matter how well written, don't fit into the story. See if you can find the problem sentences below:

Mary was thinking about her math class. She planned to spend the night studying math. First she would read the chapter. Then she would take her dog for a walk. Finally, she would do the math problems.

The rabbit sat quietly watching the cat. He remained motionless. The boy threw a ball. Finally the cat left and the rabbit hopped off.

Robert loved everything about fishing. He loved sitting in the canoe with the sun on his face. He loved to catch fish. He thought about his girlfriend. The line tightened and a fish was on the pole.

ANSWERS: Then she would take her dog for a walk. This sentence has nothing to do with Mary studying math. If taking the dog for a walk is important, remove it from the paragraph relating to Mary's math and turn it into a full paragraph. If it isn't important, delete it.

The boy threw a ball. This has nothing to do with the story about a rabbit and a cat. Either make it into it's own paragraph, or delete it.

He thought about his girlfriend. Nope, Robert was thinking about his fishing in this paragraph.

Here is another paragraph. Examine it and see if you can find the problems before looking at my answer.

Andrew was born in Milwaukee, Wisconsin. He was named Andrew after his grandfather, but his family called him Andy. His friends called him Drew. When he was a baby, Andrew slept in a bed against the wall. The wall was painted mustard yellow. Andrew was to become a football player.

ANSWER: The story begins with Andrew's birth, and his name. If this is important, the paragraph could continue talking about Andrew's name. It may tell a family story how the name had been passed down ten generations from King Andrew of Fiji. Maybe there is a story related to his nickname, Drew, which would be interesting. In short, if it's important to talk about Andrew's name, then really talk about it.

When he was a baby, Andrew slept in a bed against the wall.

What does sleeping in a bed against the wall have to do with the story? It seems to be a meaningless detail used by an insecure writer as filler. I may be wrong, there might be something very important about the bed, in which case give it the attention it deserves. Last night I heard a chilling news story related to a child's bed. It went like this:

My father was paid to collect soil and water samples from the riverbank. He stored the samples under the bed where I slept with my brothers. We slept in that bed over the water samples for years. We thought we were safe in our own home, and in our own bed. We had no idea that the water was contaminated with radioactive toxins. Now the house has been torn down, and everyone else in my family has died.

The wall was painted mustard yellow.

I then asked the writer why he was talking about mustard colored paint. Why was this important to the story? He replied that people would know the character had been poor, as only someone poor would paint a wall that color. Did you catch the meaning? I missed it, too. If you are writing about a poor character, spend time describing the wall so the writer will catch the meaning. Here is a possible paragraph.

My father painted my room mustard yellow. He had wanted to paint it sky blue and paste wallpaper giraffes along the wall, but the only color on the discount shelf was mustard yellow. The giraffe wallpaper would have cost him a month's wages at his job digging ditches, and with five mouths to feed, it was as impossible a dream as having my own bed would have been. The cheap lead-based paint peeled, and became my only toy.

Andrew was to become a football player.

The most serious problem with this sentence is that it deserves several paragraphs, not one sentence. This may be the main topic of the story but there's so much unrelated information in just one paragraph that the main topic is lost. Remember, never write less than one paragraph per idea. Children may come cheaper by the dozen, but a dozen ideas need at least twelve paragraphs.

Did you notice that "Andrew was to become" is a passive sentence? An active sentence would read: Andrew will become a football player when he grows up. Make it a habit to always look for writing mistakes that slip in and weaken a story.

SUMMARY: When I look at the paragraph about Andrew, I have no idea what idea the author is trying to portray. He is all over the place with multiple ideas. Keep your writing tight. I gave this writer the following advice: don't use any more words than you need, and don't drift with numerous ideas in one paragraph. Make sure each sentence is related to the one before, and each paragraph connects smoothly to the previous one. Techniques for transitions include using connecting words such as "however," "therefore," "and," "but," "for example," or "in conclusion." Use overlapping sentences frequently. When you are talking about a cat, have the cat notice a bird before going into the next paragraph about the bird. The change from the cat to the bird will flow smoothly and naturally. The writer will stay focused on the story, and not on the writing.

SCENES

Each scene is one section of the story. The characters are together on stage, in one place and doing one thing. A scene has action, a beginning, middle, and an end. It may consist of one or two pages, or a full chapter. Just as with writing sentences or paragraphs, it's important to have enough overlap between scenes to have them smoothly transition into each other. Make sure that one scene doesn't end so abruptly that you jar the reader out of the story. Changing scenes in books are usually marked with a white space, stars or dots, or a new chapter.

ASSIGNMENT: Check your work. Make sure each sentence connects to the next. Check that each paragraph is one, and only one, complete idea, and smoothly transitions into the next paragraph. It is okay to use words like "therefore" or "however," if you are careful not to overdo them. It may take you some time and work to become comfortable with transitions. Eventually, like other writing skills, this will become automatic for you. It's important to continue working on and being aware of smooth transitions.

Keep your writing tight. Make sure each sentence belongs with the others. If you aren't sure, take it out. If you describe something, make sure you have a reason for including it, and describe it fully. Don't give any one-liners. Don't expect the reader to know what you are talking about—be sure you tell them. Tell your story completely, and don't expect your readers to be mind readers.

"All of the books in the world contain no more information than is broadcast as video in a single large American city in a single year. Not all bits have equal value."

Carl Sagan

Chapter 5

FINDING A BALANCE

M any beginning writers have good story ideas, but miss the balance between important and unimportant subject matter. A friend sent me a story about her trip to China. She spent several pages writing about driving to the airport, meeting her friends in the travel group, and flying to China. Since I've driven to an airport and flown on a plane, this was information I was familiar with and didn't find interesting. Later in the story she wrote the following description of the Forbidden City:

> We went into the Forbidden City. It was lovely.

That's all? Disgusted, I stopped reading the manuscript. After making me wade through pages of uninspiring details about an airplane trip, she skipped information about China that would have been new and fascinating. I'd been cheated.

Another beginning writer wrote a detailed description of sweeping a floor. Unless it is a floor in a dirt hut, and is being swept with palm leaves, please spare me the details.

Here is an example of unneeded detail:

> The phone rang. Bob walked across the room and picked up the phone from the cradle. "Hello," he said.

Here is an improved version:

> The phone rang.
> "Hello," Bob said.

Your readers aren't stupid. They can fill in the gaps when presented with familiar activities. Here are a couple of descriptions from a world traveler and master storyteller interviewed in my book *Search for the Fountain.* In the first description, the traveler, Frank, assumes we know what a delicatessen is. He didn't need to describe what kinds of food he served, or how the sandwiches were made. In his later paragraph, he is talking about making brown sugar and rubber, processes unfamiliar to most readers. In these paragraphs, Frank gives rich detail:

> I ran the farm with my stepfather for two years after I got out of college, and then I ran it two years on my own. I did various things after that. I had a delicatessen. It started out with nothing, but people kept asking for stuff, so we kept adding.

*   *   *   *   *

> In Satarua they make brown sugar out of palm trees back in the rainforest. It's interesting because you can hear the wild birds back in there. I followed a path about half a mile into the jungle and there were a bunch of these palms the right size. They cut them in chunks about three feet long, quartered them, and then rubbed them against a spindle with spikes sticking out. They used to do it by hand, but now they have a washing machine motor using gasoline. They grind out the center of the palm, put it in a long trough and bail water from the stream. I don't know who's living upstream. It's a very small place, so the water may be all right. I don't know. They put this stuff in and let it soak until it absorbs all the water. Then they take it out, dry it, and it turns brown and makes brown sugar.

*   *   *

> The rubber trees are like sugar trees but you get sap. They scale them and put spigots in the trees. You have to take it out of the bucket every four hours or it will harden. They lay it out in sheets and dry it with a machine. It looks like the backside of a sheepskin. You see a guy on a motorcycle going along and on the back they have a pile of these long rubber sheets to sell.

ASSIGNMENT: Check over your work. Be sure your details are new and interesting to your reader. Skip over the mundane details that we all know.

SENTENCE LENGTH

Variation is the key to sentence length. You need to have a mix of both long and short sentences. A series of long sentences can make it difficult to follow the story, while short sentences chop the story up.

The following excerpt from *I Would Be Loved* includes a mixture of long, short, and average length sentences. This mixed sentence length adds interest and readability to the story. It also keeps the reader focused on the story, not the writing. Too many long or short sentences draw attention to themselves, and away from the story:

Then, scrunching up her funny little face in an attempt to look scary, Rosey continued, "Ghost say roar, roar, roar." She shook her hands up and down. "Ghost get me, oh, no!" Her eyes were wide in mock fear. I gave Rosey a big hug. What a wonderful story from a little girl who could barely talk six weeks earlier.

Here is one more example of varying sentence length:

Winter was approaching fast. One chilly Saturday morning the kids were home from school, playing inside, watching cartoons and just lazily wasting the day away.

Sentence length can be used to control your story's speed. A series of long sentences are useful for slowing the story down. Compare this to the music in a horror movie. The pace is slow, and we are waiting for something to happen. A series of short sentences increase the speed, just as do short choppy shots in a movie. Here is an example where I strung several short sentences together to set a fast pace, and then slowed the story and gave the reader a breath with a couple longer sentences:

"Pixie's out of my house and I'm not letting her back in. She's in the mental hospital because she threw a hot frying pan at me. The police took her away in handcuffs—she was like a wild animal. I have two new foster children so there's no room in my house for her now," Ruth said. "Did I tell you that CPS took the last child out of my home without any notice at all? The caseworker just drove up to my house and took him. She didn't even call ahead. He was returned to his mother, but I doubt it will last long."

"I guess I'm lucky," I said. "They usually give me at least a few weeks notice."

"It's different with each caseworker." Ruth fell silent. I could see how distressed she was and I shared her concern for the child's welfare. I knew the same thing could happen to my foster children and prayed it never would.

Reading your manuscript aloud is the best way to check sentence length. Too many short, choppy sentences, or too many long-winded exposés are easier for your ear, than your eye, to catch. If you have teenagers, you can ask them to listen to you read. They will be happy to find your mistakes, and won't feel shy correcting you. If you don't have teenagers, you may be able to draft a friend to listen. It's always a good idea to tape yourself reading and listen afterwards.

PARAGRAPH LENGTH

Like sentences, paragraphs need to be varying lengths. To make your manuscript more readable, have at least two or three paragraphs per page. A large solid dark space lacking indentions makes the story visually difficult and will discourage the reader from choosing your book or reading it. Like a good meal, a written story needs to have eye appeal, and this comes from having a mixture of dark and white space on each page. The following passage from *Search for the Fountain* is broken into numerous paragraphs. The second passage is identical with the exception of being written as only one paragraph. Just looking at it, you can see that the first version has more appeal:

"I help with the Historical Society back home in Hilliard, Ohio. I'm a director with the society and take care of the buildings. There's always work out there to do. We moved a church that's over a hundred years old and built a historical village, including a schoolhouse, in our hometown. Painting and repairing the schoolhouse is almost a full time job.

We have a log cabin. We couldn't find one good log cabin, but three people donated log cabins. We tore them down, took the timbers, and built one in the village with an inside staircase and an upstairs bedroom. None of them had that. They'd sleep upstairs but they had a window up there, and a ladder. Back there in those early times, you'd crawl up the ladder, go in, and then pull the ladder in so the Indians couldn't get in. Besides the staircase, we have a fireplace in there now. It's very cozy.

The Hilliard City Museum helped us build a church. They gave us fifty thousand dollars. We earned the other monies. We have a barn with all kinds of hand tools and farm machinery from the 1800 vintage. We have a railroad depot with flashing red lights and everything. The latest thing was voting booths. Florida was having so much trouble voting, so we wanted to save one for prosperity.

I have a computer, mailing lists, and e-mail. I head up a thing called the Hilliard Reunion. I just got the invitations out last week. You'd be surprised how many people from that little town come to Florida. We'll meet down at Buddy Freddie's. This is the fifth year, and we'll have seventy-five people there just from that little town.

We're sports fans, and I am in the alumni group. We've traveled around the Southwest, Midwest, Wisconsin, and Minnesota to all the Big Ten university football games. We've been to all the universities at least once, some many times during football season."

*   *   *   *   *

"I help with the Historical Society back home in Hilliard, Ohio. I'm a director with the society and take care of the buildings. There's always work out there to do. We moved a church that's over a hundred years old and built a historical village, including a schoolhouse, in our hometown. Painting and repairing the schoolhouse is almost a full time job. We have a log cabin. We couldn't find one good log cabin, but three people donated log cabins. We tore them down, took the timbers, and built one in the village with an inside staircase and an upstairs bedroom. None of them had that. They'd sleep upstairs but they had a window up there, and a ladder. Back there in those early times, you'd crawl up the ladder, go in, and then pull the ladder in so the Indians couldn't get in. Besides the staircase, we have a fireplace in there now. It's very cozy. The Hilliard City Museum helped us build a church. They gave us fifty thousand dollars. We earned the other monies. We have a barn with all kinds of hand tools and farm machinery from the 1800 vintage. We have a railroad depot with flashing red lights and everything. The latest thing was voting booths. Florida was having so much trouble voting, so we wanted to save one for prosperity. I have a computer, mailing lists, and e-mail. I head up a thing called the Hilliard Reunion. I just got the invitations out last week. You'd be surprised how many people from that little town come to Florida. We'll meet down at Buddy Freddie's. This is the fifth year, and we'll have seventy-five people there just from that little town. We're sports fans, and I am in the alumni group. We've traveled around the Southwest, Midwest, Wisconsin, and Minnesota to all the Big Ten university football games. We've been to all the universities at least once, some many times during football season."

*   *   *

SUMMARY: Always examine each page to see if there is a comfortable mixture of black and white. Good writing is more than a good story—it needs to be easy on the eye. Giving your reader eyestrain is number two on my mortal sin list, just behind being boring. This isn't limited to stories or books, either. Even a one-page letter needs to have a comfortable mixture of long and short sentences, and eye appeal that comes from balanced black and white spaces.

Chapter 6

BRINGING YOUR CHARACTERS TO LIFE

Every character, even the most fictional, has a real live person within itself. Without a touch of humanity, the reader wouldn't be able to relate to your character. Science fiction characters from far away worlds may be made of rock, or gas, or goo, but no matter, the thing that makes characters interesting to readers is that they can relate to this character on a personal level. Goolooo may have blue fur and drip, but he does things that are human, and he has the same feelings and problems that you do.

Make sure your characters are original. Captain Kirk meets Bugs Bunny may be an original combination, but these characters aren't yours. Using them is plagiarism. They're probably copyrighted and the owners are going to want boodles of money. Won't it be easier to write original characters? Is it fear that keeps you from writing characters, or maybe just the idea that you don't know this person? Meeting new people (or characters) has an element of terror for many people.

Don't worry. Before writing about a character, it is important to interview her (or him, if you insist on political correctness) and become friends. Sit down with each character over a cup of tea or coffee at your local busy fast food or coffee shop, relax, and begin interviewing your new friend. Be sure you bring your paper and pen, as you'll want to take notes. First, make sure you know what this character looks like. How tall is he, or she? How old? What features make him unique? Does he wear his hair in a ponytail? Does she have a huge nose? How does your character dress? Give exact details, using showing rather than telling (chapter 3). You might want to look around at the customers walking in and out to see if anybody there reminds you of Goolooo. Remember when you observed people and wrote about them in chapter one? Now you are writing about your own characters, but if someone just happens to have a resemblance to Goolooo, don't hesitate to take a peek at their schnoz while describing Goolooo's overgrown proboscis. Now you want to ask Goolooo about his family. What were his parents like? How many siblings does he have? Was he the oldest, middle, or youngest child, and what was that like? Where was he born? What about his childhood and education? What practical jokes did he play as a child—or as an adult? What kind of job does he do? Is he married? Kids? Who are his friends? What are his political and religious beliefs? What are his favorite foods, and what foods can't he stand? Hobbies? His family skeletons? Bad habits? Does he read, and if so, what books does he enjoy? Does he watch TV? What is his favorite movie? What are his strengths, and weaknesses? What are his passions?

Take your note pad, and favorite pen, relax, and watch the people around you. Then put your pen onto the paper and start talking to Goolooo. As you ask him questions, you will find that Goolooo answers them—ever play Ouija? This works on the same principle—your hand is only an object to hold the pen. Your characters will come alive and surprise you if you let them.

You may find out that inventing characters isn't as difficult as keeping them in line with the story. Characters have a tendency to take surprising paths that you hadn't planned or expected. Like renting a horse for a day, it's important to have a starting place and to know where you want to end up, but give your characters free rein and you will find the trip more enjoyable than if you had planned or tried to control every step.

If you have never written before, you might find the idea that characters have their own life amusing, or even silly. But even if you don't use 95% of the information your character shares with you, just having it will help your character become a fuller person in your mind, and in your writing.

About now you might be shaking your head and wondering if I'm writing this from a nut house (Oops, there I go being politically incorrect again. Not only is no offense meant, but I deny having ever said that. It must have come from one of my characters). However, once you start writing, you will experience your characters coming alive. While writing, you may spend months, or even years with these guys, so you might as well get to know them and enjoy their company. Your friends will shake their heads and keep their distance until you complete your book, and regain your sanity, but writers will understand.

NOTE: When you find that your friends always have other plans, and roll their eyes when you begin talking about Goolooo's most recent adventure (only talk about this AFTER you have written it), you might consider joining a writers' group and making friends with people who will call you and ask "How is Goolooo this morning?"

AVOID COCKTAIL PARTY INTRODUCTIONS

When you go to a cocktail party, you may be introduced to several people all at once. This does *not* result in getting to know more people, but rather in not knowing anybody because you were given too many names at the same time. You end up being confused, blaming your bad memory, and feeling uncomfortable about the situation. Since you don't want your readers to feel bad about your book, or confused about your characters, give each one enough introduction to be memorable. If the character isn't important enough to describe, you may want to reconsider whether you need this character at all. Suppose you are talking about president Z and his committee: Rodl, Eofd, ldfi, Fgoask, and Gsolid. Unless you plan to introduce each character, you might be best to say: President Z and his committee of five individuals. Then if you need to use these characters, introduce them, one at a time. You may want to use conversation with beats, inner thoughts, and exposition, (I will explain these later in this chapter) to describe each character.

"I disagree with you, Z." Rodl pulled the last purple hair out of his head and added it to the pile of hair that used to be a part of his body. Rodl looked at the pile resulting from his nervous habit. No matter, they'd grow back in a few days, and this habit wasn't any worse than the humans biting their nails. Human nail chewing puzzled Rodl, as nails were the most tasteless part of the humans. "I think it would be better to store the humans in the refrigerator than to eat them all at once in a drunken orgy," Rodl said.

Be sure to give enough attention to all the characters you introduce to make them memorable in some way. Balance the amount of description with the character's importance. Minor characters need only a sketchy introduction, while major characters need ongoing development, rather than one single long description.

POINT OF VIEW

Before you begin writing, you need to decide who will be telling the story. You can have an omniscient, third person, storyteller who sees all and knows all. This is an advantage in that the narrator can tell you what is in everyone's mind, but it has the disadvantage of being distant from every character as well.

As Goolooo walked through the woods, he was thinking about the party he planned to attend that evening. He was unaware that his archenemy, Oyez, planned to crash the party and had asked Goolooo's friend, Lysol, to help him.

At that very moment, Lysol was walking through the woods and thinking about the party. He unexpectedly met Goolooo in the woods. "Howdy" Lysol said nervously, wondering if Goolooo knew his evil plan.

As an alternative, you may have a limited, third person point of view. In this case, the outside storyteller is only aware of one or two characters. Notice that unlike the first paragraphs, this one stays in Goolooo's head and the perceptions of Lysol are Goolooo's, not the narrator's.

As Goolooo walked through the woods, he was thinking about the party he planned to attend that evening. When he met Lysol in the woods, he noticed how uncomfortable Lysol appeared, and wondered why.

We rarely hear about second person because it's irritating and is almost never used. Second person uses "you" as in "you did this," rather than "I," or "he/she".

First person narrative allows the individual to use the word "I". It's a personal story, as though we are eavesdropping into the characters head, or maybe reading his diary. The feeling is immediate, even though we are limited to the character's knowledge.

I was walking in the woods thinking about my birthday party when I ran into Lysol. He looked at me strangely, as though he was embarrassed by my presence. I wondered what was going on.

Although it's all right to change point of view, never change it within one paragraph, as this will confuse the reader. If Goolooo is telling the story in sentence one, don't have Lysol tell sentence two. Consistency in point of view is important for writing a clear and understandable story. It's best, unless you have a good reason to do otherwise, to keep the same point of view for the full scene.

In addition to point of view, you need to decide if you are writing the story in present or past tense. While most writing is done in past tense, I sometimes write in present tense to give a feeling of immediacy. I do this when I want the reader to feel as though he is there, interviewing the character along with me. The following excerpt from *Americans Lost* is an interview with a homeless man written in present tense:

Hawk has the classical appearance that many people think of when they consider what a homeless person looks like: tanned leathery skin, a long shaggy beard, old pants partially falling off his bony frame, a grocery cart overflowing with old clothes and garbage bags filled with cans. I would not have approached him without a good reason, but a mutual acquaintance, a friend of my foster daughter, Pixie, has set up this interview. However, Hawk doesn't take long to destroy my stereotype of homeless people.

"Hello." He offers me his hand and a toothless grin. "I give things away, and I pick up cans."

We shake hands and I notice that, in spite of his unkept appearance, he is washed, his clothes are clean, and his polished shoes look new. His conversation, although a bit rambling at times, is that of an educated and intelligent person fully in charge of his faculties.

GOOD GUYS, BAD GUYS

When I was an adolescent, I loved Edger Rice Burroughs. I read every Tarzan book I could find, and then moved onto his books about the Center of the Earth. Before I got to his John Carter on Mars series, I began to outgrow Burroughs. I lost interest due to the one-sidedness of his characters. Tarzan was good. He was one hundred percent good. Tarzan had no flaws, and could never make a mistake. His archenemies were bad. They were all bad. They had no redeeming features.

Modern readers won't accept these one-sided characters. Nobody is all bad, or all good. You may want to have a hero and a villain in your story, but give the hero some flaws, and allow the villain some redeeming features. In my career as a counselor, I have met many wonderful, charming people, who also happened to be robbers or murderers. You need balance to make your characters believable. Avoid one-sided, flat individuals. This is one reason why it is necessary for you to know as much as you can about your characters before you begin writing.

CHANGE

It's important that your characters change over time. If they are the same people at the end of the story as were at the beginning, the reader will wonder what the point was. Everyone learns and changes due to maturity and new experiences. Be sure you allow your characters to grow, learn, and change throughout the book. I often find that adventure stories fall flat for me when the only change occurs in the equipment. A lot of things are smashed, or a lot of people killed, but the primary character remains static, and is uninfluenced by his adventures. Even in an adventure story, people need to grow.

Change is necessary, but be sure to make it realistic. I recently read a book where one of the main characters treated other people in a cold, uncaring manner. He dragged his girlfriend around the adventure, but showed no love or caring for her. At the end, when she was about to leave him, he promised to change his ways. They hugged, kissed, and she stayed with him.

I didn't find it believable, and decided he was just pulling another con job. Characters change, but their basic personality traits, what makes them tick, can't make a sudden radical shift like that and be believable. Having him start out being a jerk, but gradually change, showing how hard he was working to become a nice guy, would have made the story stronger and more believable.

People don't necessarily improve as the story goes along. Your character can have a heart attack, become a bitter person, have his family and friends abandon him, and finally die alone and abandoned. The important thing isn't the happy ending, but believable change.

AVOID MAGICAL ENDINGS

Never use a dream ending to get out of the story by having the character suddenly wake up. If you want to have him sleeping, have him resolve his problems before waking up. The Wizard of Oz would never have become famous and loved if Dorothy had woken up while in the witch's castle. That would have resulted in readers being disappointed and disgusted. Dorothy didn't wake up until after she had found her way home, and the story was complete. Never use a dream, prayer, beam-out, or other magical situation to get your character out of a tight space. They have to resolve their problems in a believable manner.

If you want to use a coincidence, have it go against the character instead of for him. If he's worrying about losing his house because he can't pay the mortgage, and suddenly finds a bag of money, make it stolen money, and have him arrested and put in jail for robbing a bank.

AVOID EXPOSITION

Exposition occurs when a narrator interrupts the action to tell the story. Sometimes a little may be needed, but try to avoid exposition as much as possible. Here is an example of unneeded exposition.

"Mom, I don't know what we can do about our sixteen year old daughter, Katie." Pa said.

Agnes was as worried about her sixteen-year-old daughter, Katie, as was Buddy, or Pa as everyone called him. Katie had been running around with a thirty-year-old man, Fred, for the past year. Agnes was also concerned about how this would affect her three other children.

When you rewrite your story, look for exposition and remove as much as you possibly can. Rather than having the author step in and tell the story, work on showing it. You wouldn't enjoy a play or television show if a narrator stood in the background and explained the story as it happened. Your audience is intelligent, and if you do a good job of showing, they will understand the story without you standing behind their shoulder and explaining what you meant to write.

TAGS

Tags are used to show which character is talking. The simplest and most effective tag is "said."

"I'm going to the store," Alice said.

"Said," is an excellent tag to use, as it tends to disappear into the story. Using a wide variety of tags only brings attention to the tags, and marks the writer as inexperienced. There are also tags that are impossible to accomplish. When people talk, they say words. They don't laugh words, or cry words, or hiss words. That's an impossible feat. Here are some examples of tags that will draw attention to themselves, and thus away from the story.

"That's so funny," she laughed.
"I'm sorry your brother died," he cried.
"Watch out for the horn," he blared.
"I've got plans to murder her," he chuckled.
"The food is caught in my throat," he gasped.

If you are determined to do so, you can make these sentences even worse by adding adverbs:

"That's so funny," she laughed hysterically.
"I'm sorry your brother died," he cried sadly.
"Watch out for the horn," he blared loudly.
"I've got plans to murder her," he chuckled evilly.
"The food is caught in my throat," he gasped breathlessly.

On the rare occasions when you choose to use a tag other than "said" or "stated," it's important to make it a separate sentence, as this keeps people from laughing or crying words. It's a subtle grammatical change from a comma to a period, to make one sentence into two sentences.

"That's so funny." She laughed.
"I'm sorry your brother died." He cried.
"I've got plans to murder her." He chuckled.
"The food is caught in my throat." He gasped.

It's best to use tags sparingly, and leave out the adverbs. Tags weaken dialog because they tell rather than show. To show the dialog, you need to add action. This action within dialog is called beats, and replaces tags and adverbs. You won't want to take out every "said," but intermixing beats with "said" gives a comfortable balance and keeps the dialog moving. Here are the above sentences written again using beats:

"That's so funny." **She grabbed** her stomach and **laughed** until her **face turned red**.
"I'm sorry your brother died." Brad **covered his face with his hands, and attempted to stifle his tears.**
"I've got plans to murder her." Robert **chuckled** as he **picked up the sharpened knife**.
"The food is caught in my throat." David's **face turned blue** and he **grabbed his throat**.

Here is a paragraph from *I Would Be Loved* showing a beat in bold print, but also showing an error using "said," which is an unnecessary tag in this situation:

"It's been three days. You have to move her out today. I can't have her hurting my other children. I wish I didn't have to do this," I said while **untangling the phone cord** Tara had tied into knots.

This sentence would read better if I changed it to:

"It's been three days. You have to move her out today. I can't have her hurting my other children. I wish I didn't have to do this." I untangled the phone cord Tara had tied into knots.

The second version is crisper and reads better. Removing the tag, and having the beat stand alone, draws the reader into the story.

ASSIGNMENT: Go back to your story. Examine the dialog. Look for repetition. Make sure each word moves the story ahead. Look for tags, and look for places where you can replace them with beats. Remove tags that draw attention to themselves. Remove "ly" adverbs.

CONVERSATION

Conversation is what people do when they talk to each other. If you have been writing down exactly what you hear people say, that is conversation. Dialog is a written format meant to sound like conversation. Conversation rambles, is filled with stutters, ums, ahs, and hesitations, while dialog lacks these unintentional interruptions. Conversation often contains social greetings and speech that would bore a reader. Here is an example of conversation in writing:

"How are you?"
"I'm fine."
"What's new?"
"Um. Nothing much. How about you?"
"Okay."

DIALOG

Dialog is writing meant to simulate conversation. The repetitions, dysfluencies such as "um" and "ah," and generally meaningless chatter, are removed. Good dialog moves the story forward. It's important to keep in mind why your characters are talking, and where the conversation is going. In real life we ramble, but characters in a book need to be direct. They are speaking with a purpose. The purpose doesn't need to be obvious to the reader, but when you are writing conversation, you must know where your story is going, and what you want to communicate to the reader.

Don't use dialog just to feed the reader information. If you do this, conversation will sound contrived and laughable. An example of this might be:

"Our sixteen year old daughter, Katie, is out with her boyfriend, Fred, every night and he's thirty-five years old," Agnes told her husband Buddy. "I think it's a bad influence on our other children, five-year-old Missy, eight-year-old Bobby, and eleven-year-old Crissy."

Dialog needs to sound natural and believable. It should never sound forced, and the characters aren't talking just to fill you in about themselves. When you are discussing your children with your partner, you don't mention all their names and ages. You assume he knows this information. Don't have your characters do this either. If your reader needs this information, you could use a third party. Old Aunt Dorothy could come for a visit and exclaim:

"My Bobby, you have grown so much. It's hard to believe you're already eight years old. The last time I saw you, I changed your diaper."

"I'm Missy." The little girl held up five fingers. "I'm this old." (Notice I used a beat, rather than a tag).

FORESHADOWING

In the beginning and middle of your book, you will need to foreshadow future events, or characters who will appear later. This will make your story more believable, and prevent the reader from being startled or confused by a sudden, unexpected turn in the story. As with true life, one event flows from earlier events, and doesn't just suddenly happen. If you are going to have a character lose two hundred pounds and win a beauty contest, it's important to let the readers know she's gone on a diet and joined an exercise club. Be sure to prepare the reader through foreshadowing.

Foreshadowing can be subtle, or it can be obvious. Here are a couple of examples from *I Would Be Loved:*

The bathroom stall was built with tiles that started at the top of the ceiling and continued to the floor. The stall was not only completely closed in like a box, but small and poorly lit. When I tried taking her into it, Rosey turned pale and began crying. I had never seen her so frightened before.

"No go there!" NO!" she screamed in panic.

I was stunned. What had happened to her? Why was she so terrified?

This foreshadowing is obvious. The reader is waiting, and expecting the author to answer these questions. However, don't answer the questions immediately; let the reader forget them. Later, when the questions are answered, the reader will remember the earlier incident, and find it believable.

The hours passed quickly. During the coffee break, I talked to the couple sitting next to me. Ruth and Joseph were returning to foster care after having quit some time earlier. They had experience working with emotionally disturbed teenagers and wanted to care for adolescents again.

This foreshadowing isn't obvious. The reader has no idea that a hundred pages later, Ruth and Joseph will reappear when I meet their emotionally disturbed foster daughter and she becomes a major character in the story.

ENJOY YOUR WORDS—HAVE FUN

It's important to have fun with the vocabulary. English is a language rich with fascinating words, and creative ways to put them together. As children, we all spent time learning tongue twisters. "Peter Piper picked a peck of pickled peppers," is part of our culture. Unless you are Dr. Seuss, I don't suggest writing too many tongue twisters into your story, but sounds are important and enjoyable. While describing characters who behaved immaturely, I called them "Pixie," "Patty," and "Peter Pan," the children who wouldn't grow up. I had already chosen "Pixie" as the name for a main character, but chose "Patty" because I wanted another name that began and ended with the same sound. We all know "Peter Pan," so the comparison gave us a good idea what "Pixie" and "Patty" were like. I was enjoying playing with sounds. In the same manner, I recently heard a speech where the words "Ginsberg," "Goldberg," and "iceberg" were used several times. The resulting speech was both enjoyable and humorous. Another author effectively used the words "depression," "oppression," and "expression" to describe his experience as a black man in a white society.

BE EXACT

Always be careful to use exactly the word you mean. Unless you are attempting comedy, don't over exaggerate or under exaggerate your words. A leaking roof isn't catastrophic. It may be inconvenient or upsetting, but not catastrophic. The hurricane that blew your house away *is* catastrophic, not bothersome. The wonderful thing about writing is that you have the luxury of time. You can continue your story, and come back later when you think of that perfect word which eluded you the first time around. You can take the time to look through a thesaurus, or talk to a friend if you are still stuck. Sometimes it may take a third, fourth, or even a fifth proofreading before you find that perfect word.

PARALLEL SENTENCES

Parallel sentences that are used to tie two ideas together, such as; the "sky is blue, the grass is green" can make effective comparisons. Parallel sentences are often used in songs. "This land is your land, this land is my land," or "that's here, that's home, that's us," are other examples of using parallel sentences.

Don't forget to compare and contrast when describing something. The word "like," can be used to introduce a simile, and is an effective tool in describing one thing as being like another thing. Here are a few examples:

You don't teach class **like** you feed a pen of steers, take it out and throw it in. Each one of those kids is an individual.

The dog dug holes **like** bomb craters in the ground.

The amount of the miles I'm flying is **like** going to the moon every so often.

Her story was **like** peeling the layers of an onion. With each layer removed, there were tears.

The ice is two to four feet thick and when that's thawing, the drifting wind pushes the ice, and it sounds **like** thunder.

A metaphor describes something as something else. The boy isn't like an apple, as in a simile, but he actually becomes an apple. Here are a few examples:

The class isn't a pen of steers you can throw food to. Each one of those kids is an individual.

The dog dug bomb craters in the backyard.

I fly to the moon every once in a while.

Her life was an onion, and she peeled the layers as she spoke.

The ice is two to four feet thick and when that's thawing, the drifting wind pushes the ice, and it becomes thunder.

Metaphors, similes, parallel sentences, and word play will enrich your story. Creative word usage is fun for both the writer and the reader. Fluency in the English language is a gift that many people worldwide strive for. Enjoy your words.

USE SENSES

It's important to use all your senses when writing. Let your reader see, hear, smell, touch, and taste as you write. Use colors, scents, sounds, and movement to bring the story alive. Here are some travel stories from *Search for the Fountain*, which demonstrate excellent use of senses and action to bring the reader into the story:

India was filthy. Bombay, I wouldn't go back.

I became friends with the man sitting next to me on a plane. He said, "I guess we're getting close enough that we can smell Bombay."

At five thousand feet, the odor of Bombay is so strong that it gets into the plane, and you can smell it. The odor was from garbage and trash in the streets. Big white cattle wander around the city dumping on the street all the time. Nobody cleans it up.

We saw the Queen's gate. When Queen Elizabeth went to Bombay way back, they built an immense hotel, five or six stories high, and they built a huge gateway. It wasn't a gate for a person but for fourteen teams of horses to go through side by side. It was on a dock, right where the Queen got off the boat. While we were there we took a boat ride around the harbor and military base and looked at the ships.

There was a window looking out, and there was a little courtyard. There were ducks, chickens, and roosters who talked in the morning and woke everybody up.

You never think of Singapore as a big city. There are only forty to fifty acres. It's tiny. They have a big park that I didn't get to see because I didn't have enough time, but I did go through the town, and it's spic and span. If you blow an automobile horn without a good excuse, you're arrested. They don't want the noise.

The plane is going over a hundred miles an hour ahead of you, and you're under the wing. The tail is high, so if you hesitate, and can't get out, or if you catch your foot, there's no possibility that the plane will come along and hit you. You're safe from that point of view. Okay, we walked over to the door, and I stepped out. I felt sure as hel! I'd fallen forty feet onto a concrete floor—WHAM! That air hits you. You fall alone 118 miles an hour. I just looked around. It was a clear blue sky, little puffy white clouds, not clouds you pull into or anything. Pretty quickly my trainer says to me, "Put your arms out." You're supposed to have your arms out and your legs spread, so I did. We're falling.

THE TITLE

Don't worry too much about the title. You may want a "working title," something to call your work while you write it. By the time you have finished, you will have found the perfect title. Something in your story will yell at you, and you'll know what to call your book.

Somebody else might have thought of the same title as you did, especially if you borrowed the title from another source. As long as you haven't used the same title for the same subject, it's all right to have the same title repeated. You may want to write a book about a town that is swept up by a hurricane and name it Gone with the Wind. However, but don't write a love story placed in the Civil War South and title it Gone with the Wind. That's been done.

I've found that deciding the title before writing the book helps me focus on the topic. I have also changed every title I've begun with, often several times, before settling on the final name. If you don't have a title, don't let that stop you from writing. Perfect titles are like fine wine—they take time to mature.

"People who like this sort of thing
will find this the sort of thing they like."

Abraham Lincoln, in a book review

Chapter 7

YOUR AUDIENCE

Before you begin planning your story, you have to make an important decision. Who will be reading my book? No, not everybody in the world—you have to narrow it down a little bit. Actually, you have to narrow it down a lot. First you have to decide if you are writing to adults, adolescents, children, or toddlers. Is your book fiction or non-fiction? Are you writing your book to men or women, and what age group? You may decide that you are writing your memoirs for your family, or you may want a larger audience. Books are classified by fiction/nonfiction, and then by subject. There is history, science fiction, romance, mystery, adventure, religious, self-help, and dozens of other categories.

Having a clear idea of your audience is as important as having a clear idea of your characters. It is unlikely that a book on childbirth is going to draw a large audience of retired people, or that an advanced calculus book will interest children.

Be careful about the language your characters use. Hoppy the Bunny isn't going to use the same words, or thoughts, as Mr. Washington, the genius scientist. And be careful what words you use. If you are writing a book to children, keep the language at their level, or slightly above. Don't write a children's book using college level vocabulary and expect children to understand it. In the same thought, if you are writing to a college-educated audience, you need to use an adult vocabulary. Make sure that your vocabulary matches your intended audience, but always remember that at all levels, short and simple is best. Don't use complicated or difficult words to impress your audience with your intelligence.

They will be more impressed with your simple, clear writing style that makes reading effortless. This type of writing may be effortless for the reader, but it is hard work for the writer. Good writing isn't easy writing.

Your next step is to decide the theme for your book. You may have a wonderful mystery story mixed with science fiction and romance, and characters that travel throughout the world on a mission of adventure, with a surprise biblical ending, but if your publisher asks for a ten-word description of your book, what are you going to say? Here are some examples of themes from my books:

Search for the Fountain: The Secret to Youthful Aging—Advice from active seniors on how to live a long, healthy life.
I Would Be Loved—Substance exposed children in foster care.
Americans Lost—Life stories told by homeless people and those who care about them.
The Magic of Writing—A simple, step-by-step, how-to book about writing for beginners.
From Shoves to Loves—How to end violence and control in your relationship, written in rhyme.

Before you write your book, you need to envision what you are going to put on the cover description. You may have twenty-five to fifty words to describe your book and encourage the reader to buy it. You need to give them a reason to pick up your book, rather than one of the two hundred similar books that are next to yours, either on bookstore shelves, or on the Internet. Even if you are only writing an autobiography for your kids, you still need a clear focus of where you're going.

Never forget, writing a book is a lot like going on a trip. You know where you are starting, and where you are ending, but expect surprises along the way. Still, without a map, you are likely to get lost and never reach your destination. Part of your map entails answering the following questions:

Who will read my book and in a few words, what is my book about? Put these answers on 3x5 cards (you should have some left over from chapter 2) so you can use them for a handy reference. It is essential to maintain a clear focus on who you are writing the book to and your subject, in ten words or less. If you lose your focus, you may become frustrated and give up before getting much written, and then become discouraged for not being able to write. However, if you have a clear focus, you'll find writing comes with less effort and more enjoyment than you had thought possible.

"History will be kind to me for I intend to write it."

Winston Churchill

Chapter 8

THE PLOT

No matter what you're writing, whether it's a short story, a full-length novel, or a term paper, you need a beginning, a middle, and an ending. You may have an outline written in extensive detail, or maybe just an idea in your head, but the day comes when you need to start. Looking at that empty paper, or empty computer screen, is the hardest part of writing in my experience. Later, if I'm not sure what I want to write, I'll start by proofreading the last pages I wrote, and by the time I come to the end, I've warmed up and am ready to write. But writing the first page. Gosh, that's hard.

Okay, just start writing. It doesn't have to be good, it just has to be ink on paper or letters on a computer screen. If you're stuck, start by copying a few pages from a book with a similar subject matter to your intended story. This isn't cheating, this is warming-up. Athletes' warm-up before exercising, and I can't speak for other writers, but I warm-up before I write.

Begin writing your opening chapter. Don't look back, and don't edit. Most likely, you're going to find that your story doesn't really start until you've written a few pages, or maybe even a chapter or two. I know this is going to sound appalling to you, but you are going to write a lot more words, and a lot more pages, than will be in your finished book. You don't keep moldy bread in your refrigerator, do you? And you can't keep moldy words in your story. You might have written some wonderful ideas, and like moldy bread, they were fresh and wonderful at one time, but if they don't fit, they have to go. Yes, you can keep an "extra work" file if it's too painful to throw them away. They may find a perfect home some day in another story—or after a few years you might decide that it's time for them to go. For the time being, just write, write, and write some more.

You've written a beginning chapter. You've introduced the main character, or characters, and set the scene. It may not seem quite right, but don't look back. If you do, you'll get stuck on rewriting and trying to improve your opening. The important part now is to let the momentum carry you into the middle of the story.

After introducing your characters and plot, you will move into the middle, or the actual story. The beginning grabbed the readers' attention and introduced them to the main characters, and now it's time for things to happen. Each writer has their own way of planning a story. Some keep their story plots in their head, others make a brief written outline, use 3 x 5 cards with notes, or write an extensive outline. You may want to try various techniques until you find what works best for you. However you do it, you need to know where your story is going. If you are driving to an unfamiliar area you need a map, and you need a story map, too. I find it helps me to write the table of contents as a guideline to where I'm going. Having this written at the top of the paper gives me a place to add ideas as I think of them. It's a bit like going to the grocery store—without a list, I tend to forget things, and buy other things that I hadn't planned to purchase.

A good story contains at least two separate stories. They may develop separately, but eventually come together as one.

Mary Jane may be teaching school, never realizing that one of her student's life is being threatened. In the end, she learns why he has been distracted, and the murderer goes after her.

Captain Smith may be busy running his space ship and studying dangerous space phenomena, while one of his crewmen is having another problem. Captain Smith depends on this crewman to push the escape button, but the crewman is in his room, distracted by his own problem. The life of the crew is dependent on Captain Smith resolving the problem and getting the crewman back to his post on time.

The heroine may be deeply in love with the hero, but he has another problem that he needs to solve before he can give her his full attention. She is upset, and leaves him for another adventure. It isn't until the end, after they both solve their separate problems, that they finally develop a relationship.

The super-being may be busy preventing a train wreck, while the love of his life is near death from the villain's evil plot.

When you read a story, or watch a movie, look for the story within the story. When you write anything longer than a short story, make sure you have two strong stories. Your stories will probably start out separately, the characters meet briefly, and then go into their own stories. An alternative possibility is that your characters know each other at the beginning, become separated, and then meet again at the end. If you are writing a short story, one story is enough, but a novel requires at least two strong stories to keep it going fifty to a hundred thousand words.

The end ties everything together. All the foreshadowing that you used in the beginning and middle of your story should now come together and culminate in the events that were foreshadowed. Your separate characters meet and resolve their problems, and all loose ends are tied together. Keep the excitement high with a lot of action, and short sentences. The end is not the place for long descriptions, or characters who ponder the meaning of life. The end is a place for action and fast reading. Finally, end the book in a believable way. Avoid magic, technology that "beams" the hero out of trouble, dreams, and even if your story has a religious emphasis, the characters need to solve their problems and never pray them away. After your main character, the protagonist, solves his problem on his own, you can have him wake-up, be beamed up, or have his prayer answered, but never use these as techniques to solve problems.

Now that you have written a possible beginning, middle, and an end, go back to the beginning. You have a better idea of how the book will turn out after having finished it. Look at your beginning and make whatever changes you need. You may need to foreshadow that character you invented on page 250, and hadn't thought about earlier. You may find that the beginning drags, and the real action doesn't begin until later. It's not only okay, but necessary to remove your slow moving beginning pages and begin with action. You need to grab the reader's attention at the beginning. If the first couple of pages are slow, it's likely your reader will close the book and never get to the exciting part. Start with the exciting part and hook your audience early.

Once your reader is hooked, keep him reading. End each chapter with a cliffhanger so he turns the page and starts the next chapter. The term cliffhanger may have come from a scene such as this:

The hero is running from a savage tribe of Indians. He runs to the edge of a cliff and begins climbing down. He grabs a branch, but he can't go down any farther without falling. He looks up and the Indians are standing there with their bows and arrows. He looks down and sees rapids and a deadly waterfall. Now he notices a beaver chewing on the branch that he is holding onto, and the branch begins to crack...

"Books are never finished they are merely abandoned."

Oscar Wilde

Chapter 9

REWRITING

You have completed your story. You have spent hundreds of hours and now you have a completed manuscript ready to publish and show the public—right? WRONG. Now the real work comes. It's time to rewrite.

Go back to the beginning. Even though you've used the computer spell-check, you need to read and check the spelling. Your computer doesn't know the difference between there, their, they're, your or you're. Your computer won't catch it hen you leave the W off "when," as I just did. A computer is a tool to help you write, but it can't, and never will, take the place of your human brain. Your brain is far more sophisticated and powerful than any computer ever will be. Check your grammar, and don't trust the computer's grammar check either. It will give you wrong information on a regular basis.

Check your writing word for word. Have you used the most succinct and exact word possible? Remove adverbs and the other common mistakes discussed in chapter two. Remove unnecessary punctuation, and redundant words or phrases that slipped in unnoticed.

Make sure your writing is tight. Look for wordy sentences that can be removed or shortened. Check the balance. Have you described only what needs to be described, and left the writer to fill-in everyday details? Check the visual appearance of the page. Make sure there is a comfortable balance between the words and white space. Check your sentence length and make sure it varies. Use shorter sentences to move the action faster, and longer sentences to slow things down and give your reader a breather.

Check your word usage. Remove clichés, idioms, and overused expressions. Include original metaphors, similes, parallel sentences, and word play.

Check your story for incidences where you told the story, when you could have shown it. This is the difference between someone else telling you something, and experiencing it for yourself. If you need more practice in this area, reread chapter three. Showing rather than telling is the difference between a story that can't be put down, and one that is put back onto the shelf unread.

Double-check your story. Make sure your facts are accurate. Check for inconsistencies. If a character is wearing a red sweater on page 10, don't have her wearing a blue jacket on page 25 unless you mention she has changed her clothes. Be careful with details—if you've changed a character's name or appearance, make sure that you have changed it throughout the book. Use a word find and replacement whenever you can to make sure you haven't missed any changes, but don't forget to use your own eyes and brain to double check.

After you have reread the story, read it again out loud. It should flow easily, and sound comfortable to your ear. Rewrite passages where you stumble, or where your words don't flow smoothly.

Once the story is as smooth as you can make it—now, and not before—it's time to share a few chapters with your writing group or a friend who loves reading. Your proofreader will help you find the mistakes that you passed over in your final rewrite. If you can afford the cost, consider having a professional editor check your work before publication.

Put as much time and attention into rewriting as you did into writing your original story. Nobody writes a perfect story the first time. The best authors in the world need to rewrite. Don't pass this up as unimportant. Most of writing is rewriting, rewriting, and rewriting. But, don't rewrite endlessly, two or three times through and you will find diminishing returns for your effort. Now it's time to sell your work, and start your next writing project.

Chapter 10

WRITING AN ARTICLE OR ESSAY

The rules for good writing don't change when you are writing non-fiction. No matter whether you are writing a letter, a term paper, a research dissertation, or a report—good writing remains the same. Always avoid passive sentences, unnecessary wordiness, and clichés. Show rather than tell whenever possible. No matter what field of study you are writing in, these rules remain the same. Even when writing a letter, careful writing counts.

When writing reports, avoid sentences such as "Mrs. Smith did show for her appointment. She was depressed. She was hospitalized." Change it to: "Mrs. Smith showed for her appointment." Instead of saying she was depressed, show how she acted. "Mrs. Smith cried through the appointment and described her plan to commit suicide." Turn the last, passive sentence into an active sentence "Dr. Jones admitted Mrs. Smith to the hospital due to severe depression."

NONFICTION WRITING

There are many more non-fiction books bought than fiction. This means that if you are serious about becoming an author, you have a better chance of being published by a royalty press if you write non-fiction rather than fiction.

There is not much difference between writing non-fiction and fiction. Both require careful research. Research is important, however, don't research so long that you never write the story. Once you stop finding new facts, and feel as though you know enough to write the articles yourself, it's time to stop researching and start writing.

The purpose of both fiction and non-fiction is to communicate ideas. Nonfiction, as well as fiction readers, appreciate well-written prose, but good writing is only a method to facilitate communication. The story, or the message, is always more important than the quality of writing. Classical books haven't survived due to excellent writing, but to their strong stories. Writing styles change over time, and classics are poorly written by today's standards. They remain classics not due to their writing, but because a good story is appreciated in any generation.

TEXTBOOKS

Although nonfiction books emphasize information, this isn't an excuse for poor writing. Textbooks are notorious for poor writing. There are textbooks that primarily use passive sentences. Too many textbook authors seem to love long convoluted sentences and difficult words. Be honest, how often do you read textbooks for enjoyment? Far too many students plow through a chapter or two, and then give up with frustration. Even if you are writing a textbook, if you want your readers to understand and finish your book, follow the rules for good writing.

JARGON

Each professional field has it's own jargon. The purpose of jargon is to clarify and shorten your writing, not to impress readers with how intelligent you are, or to make your writing complicated and difficult to understand. Always use the simplest and shortest word possible. If one word of jargon can take the place of a sentence or two, then using it is correct. "Dementia" is shorter and easier to say that "loss of mental capacity." Sometimes jargon takes the place of a politically incorrect word, such as using "dementia" rather than "senile".

There are authors who rely on jargon, but always remember, the reason for jargon (or any writing for that matter) isn't to impress someone with your huge vocabulary, but to communicate as clearly and simply as possible. Use jargon only when it's the clearest way to communicate, and is a word that you know will be familiar to your readers. If you are unsure whether or not your readers will be familiar with specific jargon, either define it, or delete it.

FORMAT

Whether you are writing a letter, a term paper, or a dissertation, you must follow a specified format. The various formats you must use are beyond the scope of this book. There are numerous books which demonstrate specific formats. They may show details as exact as where to use periods and commas in bibliographies. If you are working in a professional field, be sure to consult the specific publication manual that describes the writing style you must follow.

TOPIC

Before writing a paper, you need to determine your topic. It's important to limit your topic to one subject. Writing about the United States of America would be impossibly complicated, and far too much for one paper, and even too much for a book. Writing about Florida is still too much. You need to narrow your topic to a manageable size. You might want to write about a political election in Miami, problems with alligators, sinkholes, or the effects of human population growth on the water table in central Florida. Whatever you choose to write about, make sure you have a clear focus. Once you have your focus, the paper will flow smoothly, and writing will become easy. Make sure you develop points which always go back to your topic. If you are writing about alligator problems in Florida, make sure each point relates to alligator problems. You may want to talk about how people are moving into alligators' environment, how people endanger alligators, and how alligators are dangerous to people. This paper doesn't have any place for describing in detail how alligators were a species before dinosaurs. This is off the topic of alligators and people.

PURPOSE

You need to have a clear purpose to your paper. You may try to persuade people to believe as you do, explain how something happens, or educate people on a specific topic. Without a purpose, your paper is likely to ramble and be difficult to write. Knowing your purpose, along with your topic, will prevent you from getting stuck, or developing writer's block.

OUTLINE

An outline is essential for writing an essay or research paper. A good outline will help you focus on where your paper is going. This kind of writing differs from fiction writing in that you must remain in control at all times. You can't just write the beginning and end and create a free-flowing middle as you go—you must retain strict control over your writing throughout a paper. Outlines differ.

Some people work well with just a few notes, while others need detailed, formal outlines. There is no right or wrong way, so choose the method that is best for you. If a formal outline is needed as part of your paper, consult the publication guide specific to your research field for details on how to write this.

BODY

After developing an outline and topic, you will want to skip the introduction, and begin with the body. Each paragraph in your body needs to start with one main idea, next give ideas to support the main idea, and finally, the ideas are expanded and elaborated on. Here is an example:

Main idea: Alligators and humans are not compatible, and endanger each other.
Supporting point: Humans are taking over their land.
Elaboration: Humans are building homes in the alligator's habitat, swamps where they live are being drained, and people disturb the animals that alligators eat.
Second supporting point: Humans are dangerous to alligators.
Elaboration: Not only do humans destroy alligators' habitat, but they are directly dangerous to alligators. Hunters shoot alligators. Dogs find and destroy their eggs.
Third supporting point: Alligators are dangerous to people.
Elaboration: Alligators will attack a grown man. An alligator can eat a small child.

CONCLUSION

The conclusion sums up the article, gives a final perspective to the paper, and brings closure. A conclusion may be a few sentences, or short paragraph. You may also include a discussion of the topic. The conclusion shouldn't merely summarize the article, but it should put the ideas of the article together into one cohesive idea.

Humans and alligators aren't designed to live in the same habitat. When they come together, it means problems for both alligators and humans. Although we often consider alligators dangerous animals, humans are also a danger to alligators.

INTRODUCTION

Now that your paper is complete, it will be easy to return to the beginning and write an introduction to grab the reader's interest while introducing the topic.

When humans come in contact with prehistoric monsters, such as alligators, it is bad news. This paper will discuss the problems involved for both alligators and humans when they meet.

ABSTRACT

Although a term paper begins with an abstract, write it last. If you write it first, you are abstracting what you plan to write. Even though you may have a detailed outline, your final outcome may be somewhat different from what you planned. Wait until you've finished the paper and you will have a clear idea what your abstract, which is a brief summary of the article, should say. Here is an example from the alligator article:

This paper discusses the problems that occur when humans and alligators come in contact with each other. It deals with the dangers people cause directly to alligators, and indirectly by damaging their environment. It also explains the dangers alligators can cause to humans.

FINSHING TOUCHES

Wait a day or two (a week or longer is better) and re-read your paper. Make sure everything flows smoothly from one idea into the next. Check that the writing is tight, nothing extra is put in, and everything is described with adequate details. Make sure the abstract describes the article, and the introduction leads into the body. The conclusion shouldn't repeat the article, but brings in a new perspective to tie it all together. The main topic, or theme, of the article must be present in all sections. Check for passive sentences and change them to active sentences. Show rather than tell goes for articles as well as fiction writing.

Chapter 11

ROYALTY PUBLISHING

There are numerous reasons why people write. Some write to relax or to express their feelings. This is generally done in a diary or journal, and kept private. Writing to express feelings can be therapeutic, and I encourage you to do this if you enjoy it. There are people who have their whole life history written in diaries—volumes of books written but never shown to anybody. This type of writing is done primarily for personal expression and enjoyment.

Another type of writing is done exclusively for class or work. This is required writing, and is seen by a limited number of people. This is purposeful writing, written to meet a goal. You may enjoy this kind of writing, but many people do not care for it.

The last kind of writing is done by choice, is written for enjoyment, but is also purposeful outside one's enjoyment. Books are written for an audience, and communicate an idea, educate people on a topic, or just tell a story. The audience may be as small as your family, such as a family history, or as large as the world. Placement in bookstores, and on the Internet, is the epitome when writing for the public. Once you hold your first book in your hands, once your first book is listed on the Internet, or placed on a bookstore shelf, you'll be hooked. Now others will know what you've known since you put your first word on paper—you are a writer, and an author.

Once you finish your story, it's time to sell it. There are people who are afraid of sending their work to an agent or publisher, concerned that it may be stolen. Many stories have similar themes, so if you submit something, are turned down, and shortly after a similar story is published, that doesn't mean your story was stolen. Romeo and Juliet has been rewritten hundreds of times, and each has it's own writing and unique twist.

Although stories can be copyrighted, ideas can't. It is unlikely that an agent or publisher will steal your work. They couldn't stay in business long if they did, but if you are concerned, send yourself a copy and keep it unopened. You will then have proof that you wrote it before sending it out. If you are still concerned, it may comfort you to know that just the act of writing gives you an automatic legal copyright on your work. I will give you more information about obtaining an official copyright in the next chapter.

QUERY LETTER

The query letter is your introduction to a publisher or agent. Like all first impressions, it's a reflection of who you are. An excellent query letter is your first, and probably only chance of getting an agent or publisher to read your manuscript. Like a resume, limit your query to one, and certainly no more than two pages. Publishers are busy and read for hours. A catchy, tight letter is more likely to result in a request to see your manuscript than a longer letter.

There are several parts to a query. The first paragraph is the grabber, or hook. You need to hook the publisher or agent with your idea. If he isn't immediately intrigued, he probably won't read any further. Begin with a shocking statement, a puzzle, or a tease that makes your query difficult to put down. The query for my book *I Would be Loved*, began:

Crack Kids. This is the hot topic being reported in every newspaper in the country. The first of the "crack babies" have already entered the public school system. What are they like? How are they doing? What is the hidden story behind the headlines?

In the next paragraph, you will want to supply a little more information about your book. Write a few sentences giving the title, if your book is fiction or nonfiction, the word count and the subject. An average page is 250 words, but your computer will give you an exact count when you click on tools at the top of the page.

I have written a 57,000-word narrative nonfiction book titled *I Would Be Loved*, about my foster children who were damaged by drugs, alcohol, abuse, and by the system meant to protect them.

You will also want to introduce yourself. Describe your expertise about the subject as well as your writing experience:

In the early 1990's, I was a foster parent at the peak of the crack cocaine epidemic. Most of my children were infants, but one, Pixie, came to live with me after leaving foster care at eighteen. A chapter from this book took first prize in a writing contest sponsored by the Tampa Writer's Alliance.

If a well-known person or expert in the field you have written about has reviewed your book, or written a forward, be sure to mention it:

Patty Munter, the former President of the National Organization of Fetal Alcohol Syndrome has written a forward to my book.

You need to research the market for your subject. This can be done over the Internet, but I suggest you go to major bookstores and see what is actually on the shelves that is comparable to your topic:

Although *I Would Be Loved* is based on a true story, it reads like a novel. There are not many books available to the general public on this topic, and most are written as textbooks. *The Broken Cord*, by Michael Dorris, was the last popular book written about a child with fetal alcohol syndrome. It remained in print for years and a movie was made from it. Books presently in print, regarding the topic of foster care and substance exposed children include; *The Sexualized Child in Foster Care: A Guide for Foster Parents and Other Professionals,* by Sally G. Hoyle*; Fantastic Antone Grows up; Adolescents and Adults with Fetal Alcohol Syndrome,* by Judith Kleinfeld (ed), et al.; *Kids, Crack, and the Community,* by Barbara B. Kicks. Books on this topic are infrequently found in bookstores, and the market is wide open for another popular book to follow *The Broken Cord.*

Your perspective publisher or agent will need to know the audience your book is written for. This is important to them when they consider sales potential. No matter how good your book is, not everyone will buy it. You need to be clear who your target audience is, and share this information in your query letter.

I Would Be Loved would interest anyone who comes in contact with drug or alcohol exposed children. This could include teachers, professionals in medicine, speech therapy, psychology, and other fields that help disabled children. It will interest direct-care workers for these children, including foster parents, birth parents, and caretaking relatives.

You need to include ideas for marketing your book. Although this is your "baby," to the publisher, it's a business proposition.

Numerous organizations for disabled, hyperactive, and drug/alcohol-exposed children have large memberships and frequent conventions throughout the country where *I Would Be Loved* would be welcomed for display and sale.

Lastly, you need to ask their permission to send the manuscript. It's always important to send it only after it's been requested. Manuscripts that haven't been requested land in the slush pile with thousands of others, possibly to be read later, or sent back to the author unopened. Considering that the cost of printing and postage for a single manuscript can easily exceed twenty dollars, it's best to send a letter and wait for a request before sending your precious manuscript to someone who isn't interested in seeing your work. Authors get enough rejection without inviting more. Very few books in the slush pile are ever published, so don't let yours end up there. Here is my closing paragraph:

I would be happy to send you an outline, sample chapter, or the completed manuscript. I am looking forward to your response.
Sincerely,
Linda J. Falkner

Writing a good query letter may take several days, or longer, as you put it aside to cool off, and rewrite it until it is perfect. I suggest you go to the library or a bookstore and find a book with sample query letters. Taking the time to study more queries, and then making yours perfect, will pay off with increased requests to see your manuscript, and hopefully a sale.

AGENTS

There are good agents and poor agents. Check your agent's qualifications by asking what books he has sold in the past year. Always ask for his credentials and professional memberships. Two organizations, the Association of Authors' Representatives (USA) and the Association of Authors' Agents (UK), require members to adhere to codes of ethics that help ensure minimal standards of honesty, quality, and ethics. Associations also offer conferences and ongoing education regarding changes and new information relating to the publishing industry. While being affiliated with a professional organization isn't a requirement for an agent, it demonstrates a desirable attitude towards professionalism.

Be sure you have a contract that clearly spells out what your agent's responsibilities are, and what yours are. It's important that all costs are related to book sales, not the agent's time or expenses. Most agents work on commission. An agent submits manuscripts to publishers and helps with the business end of publishing. He will find you a publisher, help negotiate a better contract for you, collect your money, help resolve any problems you have with the publisher, take his percentage, which ranges from 15-20%, and send you your money.

Because many more books are represented than are actually sold, you have a better chance of being represented by an agent than you do selling your book directly to a publishing house. Some large publishing companies refuse to read a manuscript that was sent by an unknown author, and require submission through an agent. They prefer to have an agent prescreen manuscripts and discard poorly written, non-publishable work. Using an agent saves them time and money.

Having someone else submit your work can also save you time and money. While an agent is submitting your manuscript, you are free to begin writing your next book. While you are doing what you do best, which is writing, your agent will be doing what he does best, which is making contacts and promoting your manuscript. Because agents have contacts with publishers, they have a better idea of who would be interested in your work. Still, no agent can sell a weak, poorly written manuscript. If your work is good, you can sell it yourself, but you will have to invest the time and money to send query letters, and once it is requested, your manuscript, to publishers.

WARNING—Reputable agents are paid a percentage of your advance, and book sales. They don't make money until you do, and they don't charge fees for reading, or costs. Some agencies charge a reading fee. It is best to avoid an agent, or agency, that makes its money through substantial reading fees, rather than through sales.

HOW TO LOCATE AND APPROACH AN AGENT

There are numerous books available in libraries, bookstores, and over the Internet that list agents and publishers. The bible of publishing is *The Writers Market*. *The Writers Market* describes the type of work each publisher is looking for, addresses, and the contact person. Another excellent resource to locating an agent is the *Writer's Guide to Book Editors, Publishers, and Literary Agents*. These books are updated yearly. Many published books include an acknowledgement to the agent, and this is another good place to get names of agents who specialize in your specific field of writing or genre.

Once you have decided which agents you may wish to work with, you need to send query letters. Each query begins with the agent's name—Dear Joe Smith, never Dear Agent or Dear Sir.

When you send your query, you need to include a self-addressed stamped envelope, otherwise known as a SASE (pronounced sassy) so your agent can notify you that he isn't interested. If he is interested, he will ask to see your work, or your manuscript.

When he requests it (and not before), send your manuscript, addressed to him personally, in a heavy-duty stationary box. Each page should be typed on white, standard weight (20 lb.) paper and be as perfect as you can make it. With modern day spellcheckers and printers, there is no excuse to have misspelled words, white-out, or crossed out words. Handwritten work is never acceptable. Do not use colored paper, boarders, or anything else to make your manuscript stand out. The agent has requested it, and will read it. Your work must look perfect and professional. This is not the time to be flashy or creative; save that for your writing. Your manuscript must be placed in the stationary box face up with the title page showing when you open it. Never staple, bind, or paper-clip the manuscript. Each page must be loose, printed with the book title, and numbered.

If you want your manuscript returned, you must send a SASE, a self-addressed stamped mailing envelope large enough to send back your work. You may also choose to tell the agent that you don't want the manuscript returned, and he may dispose of it if he doesn't buy it.

Some people who are concerned about having their story stolen feel more comfortable having it returned. Since it costs as much to mail a manuscript back as to print a brand-new copy for the next agent who requests it, I prefer to send a clean, new copy each time, and save the postage costs. Agents and publishers are in the business of buying manuscripts and have no need or desire to steal them. Your agent isn't in the business of stealing stories, but helping you sell them.

ROYALTY PUBLISHING

There are thousands of large and small publishing houses that purchase manuscripts and pay the author a royalty up front. Some larger houses will only accept manuscripts submitted by agents, but most publishing companies will read unagented works. The publisher negotiates a contract with the author and pays an advance on future earnings. The publisher, or publishing house, buys the book rights. They become the owner, pay all publishing costs, and have control over the cover, and even the title. The publisher files a copyright with the government and procures an ISBN and LCCN number.

When trying to sell your book to a royalty press, query first. Never send your manuscript unless a publisher has read your query and requested that you send the book. Unrequested manuscripts are either returned unopened, or put on the slush pile to be read when, and if, someone has time.

It is rare that a successful book comes from the slush pile. One exception is Tom Clancy's first book, The Hunt for Red October, which was sent to a small publishing house that specializes in submarine action-adventures. It was discovered in a slush pile, published, and became a best seller. Realistically, you have a much better chance of being hit by lightening than you do of having your book discovered from that deep, dark hole of oblivion. If you want to be considered a serious, professional author, don't let your work get into a slush pile.

Using a copy of *The Writers Market*, or any other book that lists publishers' names and addresses, send query letters to each publisher that accepts work similar to yours. Don't send your query to an inappropriate agent or publisher, such as sending your mystery story to a publisher who only prints cookbooks. The procedure for sending a query to a publisher is identical to sending one to an agent. Make sure the query letter looks professional, and spend time making sure it's as perfect as you can make it. Address the query to an individual, Mr. John Smith, not Dear Sir, and don't forget to enclose a self addressed stamped envelope (SASE).

Soon your SASE's will begin filling your mailbox. I heard some excellent advice when I first began writing, and I want to share this with you—it may help keep your spirits up. You need enough rejection letters to cover a wall before you're going to sell your first book. This is a great time to start your collection. The more query letters you send, the more rejection letters will arrive for you to add to your collection. Some people collect stamps or coins, but authors, even famous ones, collect rejection letters.

One day a letter will come from a publisher using his own envelope and stamp. This will be a letter saying, "Please send your manuscript—I'd like to read it." Once the police leave (the neighbors heard you yelling so loudly they thought someone was murdering you and called 911), place a clean copy of your manuscript, typed on plain white paper, into a stationary box and send it to the publisher, addressed to the individual who requested it. The post office can supply you with a heavy-duty shipping box. The pages must be loose, *never* stapled, paper-clipped together, or bound in any way, and include a large SASE if you want your work returned.

If a royalty press accepts your work, you will sign a contract and production will begin. If you don't have an agent, you will want to hire a literary attorney to review your contract and make sure you are getting a fair deal. There are horror stories of first time authors giving away all the rights to not only their present book, but any future books they might write.

Royalties paid on these books are generally small because the publisher, and not the author, incurs the financial risk for publishing this book. Exact figures differ from one publisher to another, but 2-10% is usually paid to the author.

An advance is money the publisher pays to you when you sign the contract. This money is an interest free loan that will be subtracted from your royalties. Your first royalties will be used to pay back your advance, and you won't receive any royalties until the advance is paid back. Once thing you want your agent or attorney to do is to negotiate the largest advance possible since this may be the only money you ever earn on your book. It's important to make sure your contract doesn't require you to pay the advance back if the book doesn't earn enough royalties to cover it.

A large advance is important for a second reason. The larger the advance, the more commitment the publisher has in making this book a success. The best book in the world can't be successful if it doesn't have a prominent location in bookstores. Bookstores save the best spaces in the front for big name authors whose work they know will sell.

Once it is accepted, the contract signed, and the advance paid, it can take a year or longer for your manuscript to become a book. Then there is no guarantee that it will be placed in bookstores, or kept there for more than a few weeks. But by this time, you will be working hard on your next book, as well as developing a name and a following. Many "overnight successes" wrote for ten years or longer before being discovered. Many best selling books were turned down numerous times before finally finding a publisher willing to give them a chance.

One reason that it is difficult to get published is that publishers prefer to concentrate on the big names that guarantee them sales and money. While there are some publishers who are willing to take a chance on an unknown name, most aren't interested in taking this costly gamble on an unknown. However, while getting a publisher may be a desirable goal, not having one doesn't have to block you from publishing and selling your books.

Chapter 12

SELF-PUBLISHING

AVOID VANITY/SUBSIDY PRESSES

Vanity presses are bad news. They often advertise to "new authors," but being published by a vanity press can be worse for your future writing career than being an unknown and unpublished writer. Being published by a vanity press puts a black mark, or a stigma, on your name that is hard to remove. Publishers and bookstores treat vanity books as though they were contagious with a deadly plague.

Because vanity presses have a bad name, they changed their name, but not their sleazy practices. Now they are called "subsidy presses", but you can expect another name change in the future. I've heard that some are changing to the name "co-publishing".

Vanity presses print those advertisements you see in magazines that say writers are needed. They often offer a "free" talent test and request you send them your book. No matter how bad a book is, they send back glowing praise and an offer to publish it at a price. Vanity presses often have poetry contests. Your poem will be published in a book, conditional on you purchasing the book at an inflated price.

Vanity presses offer to buy manuscripts, and supply glowing statements about how wonderful their books are. The truth is, they charge, and usually overcharge you for every step in publishing the book. Seriously, you could buy a luxury car for the amount some charge to publish your book. Yet, after the book is published, they maintain ownership, and you are required to buy your books back from them. You've paid twice, once to publish the books at an inflated price, and now to purchase your own books.

Vanity publishers don't proofread your material, so any mistakes or poor writing stays in the book. In addition, they use cheap templates for the cover and inside print, resulting in poor quality books. As a result, once a vanity press publishes your book, it will not be able to get reviews in major newspapers. Without such a review, your sales will be limited. You can also forget about seeing your book in any mainstream bookstores, as they don't accept these books. Most likely, the only books you can expect to sell are those you personally purchase and sell.

It is always a good idea to be cautious. I recommend you hire a literary attorney, someone who specializes in book contracts, to read over any contract before signing it. Look for the word, "vanity," "subsidy," or "co-publisher". If a contract appears "too good to be true," it probably is a scam. Beware if you feel any high-pressure tactics, such as "act immediately," or "this offer expires today." Never pay someone to read your manuscript, and be suspicious of contests. Beware of anyone who wants total rights to your work, or to rights to future works. Beware of companies that give testimonials. Beware of companies that won't give you a cost estimate unless you send them your book. Beware of companies that offer you a one-dollar advance to purchase rights to your book. Beware of companies that ask for a reading fee, and be especially wary if they offer an installment, or payment plan. There are an abundance of publishing scam artists just waiting to take your money, and rights to your books, if you are willing to share with them.

INDEPENDENT OR SELF-PUBLISHING

You may want to self-publish by contracting with a publishing company who will put your manuscript into published form. Self-publishing differs from a vanity/subsidy house in that you publish and own your books. You pay the costs of putting the book into print and the publisher gives you all the copies.

The advantage of self-publishing is that you have complete control and ownership, and keep one hundred percent of the profits. You own all the copies printed, and they are sent directly to you.

There are several disadvantages to self-publishing. The initial set-up cost can be in the thousands of dollars. This isn't an option for someone on a tight budget. Once you have the books printed, you are the exclusive owner, and the books are all sent to you. You will get a better price on each book if you order a large printing than you will in a smaller printing, so you need room to store your books. Imagine how much space five hundred, one thousand, or even two thousand books will take in your house.

The next problem, and this problem is immense, is how to sell these books. Unless you have published with the intention of giving the books away free (maybe for a family reunion), you'll find them harder to sell than you expected. All those people who encouraged you to write, and promised to buy, suddenly disappear. A dedicated sales person, willing to give speeches, attend book signings, and make selling a full time job, may be able to sell three hundred books before saturating their local market. Very few self published authors ever earn back their initial investment, and many end up giving their books away after tiring of storing them for a couple of years. I suggest that unless you are a well-known person who travels and gives speeches, and can afford several thousand dollars start-up costs, self-publishing through an independent publishing, or printing company, is going to be a costly and time-consuming way to get your book into print.

If I haven't discouraged you, and you want more information, contact these websites. They can help you avoid dishonest scams, and direct you to publishers, distributors, and consultants who can help you learn the steps to self-publishing.

Small Publishers of North America http://www.spannet.org
Publishers Marketing Association http://www.pma-online.org
http://www.ad.com/Business/Publishing_and_Printing/
Self-Publishing/Book_Packager.

MISCELLANEOUS QUESTIONS

ISBN—INTERNATIONAL STANDARD BOOK NUMBER

The International Standard Book Number or ISBN is a ten-digit bar code assigned to each book used to identify the publisher and title. It is necessary to have an ISBN for the book to be published because bookstores and distributors use ISBN numbers to track inventory and sales. If you are writing a book only for your family and friends, you don't need an ISBN number. IBSN numbers are supplied upon request, but beware, some publishers will overcharge you for them. I recently found two publishing companies over the Internet offering ISBN numbers. The first one stated that they charge twenty-five dollars to cover the ISBN cost. The other one charges $115. The US ISBN agency that assigns ISBN numbers charges only a token processing fee ($1.50 as of this writing). For more information, contact the ISBN Agency at:

U.S. ISBN Agency
630 Central Avenue

New Providence, NJ 07974
Tel: 877-310-7333
Fax: 908-219-0188
isbn-san@bowker.com

LCCN—LIBRARY OF CONGRESS CONTROL NUMBER

The Library of Congress Control Number or LCCN is a number that assists libraries and bookstores when ordering. There is no charge to obtain a LCCN, but the author is obligated to send a complimentary copy of the best edition of each book to the Library of Congress upon publication. If you are planning on having libraries purchase your book, you may want to have a LCCN assigned to your book prior to publication. For more information, contact the Library of Congress at:

Library of Congress
Cataloging in Publication Division
101 Independence Ave., S.E.
Washington, D.C. 20540-4320

COPYRIGHT

Present laws consider any written material to be automatically copyrighted effective from the moment you have written it. However, if you are publishing, it's a good idea to have your work copyrighted in case you get into a lawsuit. The process if easy and inexpensive, but takes a few months to process. For more information, contact the copyright address:

Library of Congress
Copyright Office
101 Independence Avenue, S.E.
Washington, D.C.20559
Tel.: (202) 707-3000 Email: copyinfo@loc.gov

Chapter 13

PRINT ON DEMAND
AND E-BOOKS

Print on demand, or POD (pee-oh-dee), is the newest way to publish. POD is the one method that makes publication possible for anybody serious about publishing. You don't need a lot of money to get your book into POD format. You don't need to spend a lot of time selling your book to earn back your initial investment, and you don't need to store any more books that you wish. Most of all, you won't develop a new hobby pasting rejection letters to your wall while waiting for someone to buy your book. In a matter of a month or two, you can have a published book and with luck, an occasional royalty check in your mailbox. Don't expect to get rich, but it should be enough to pay for a dinner out with your friend or partner.

E-BOOKS

E-books don't exist in reality. They don't have a cover or pages, and you can't comfortably cozy-up to read an e-book in bed at night. E-books are available over computers, and when someone orders and pays for an e-book, it is downloaded directly onto their computer. Most POD companies offer e-book options. If the cost is nominal, it does no harm to purchase this option, but if the POD charges you a high fee, I don't suggest it. Very few people buy e-books, as most readers still prefer having a real book to read. However, since new technology includes small pocket computers designed to download books, e-book sales may increase in the future, and become a viable option to bookselling.

PRINT ON DEMAND (POD)

Print on Demand companies publish books one at a time after they are ordered and paid for. The author pays for the initial set-up costs to put the book into a publishable format, but not for the actual printing. For this reason, POD books cost much less to self-publish than any other method. POD fees have increased over the past couple of years, but you can still expect your expenses to be in a few hundred-dollar range, and even the most deluxe packages rarely run over a thousand dollars. Generally, but not always, the higher costing packages pay a higher royalty.

Print on Demand books are sold over the Internet or are ordered through bookstores. They are sent directly to the person purchasing the book, or to the bookstore. When someone orders a book over your website, a POD site, or major bookstore such as Amazon.com, Barnes & Nobles, or Booksamillion, payment is procured through a credit card or bankcard with a credit card logo. The book is then printed and sent to the purchaser. The printing company is paid, the POD company takes an agreed upon share, and the remainder is sent to the author.

Because books published through Print on Demand companies are printed only after they are sold, there are no storage costs. The POD publisher is willing to publish an unknown work, or a work that is intended for only a few people (such as a book about your life written only for your children), because you pay the set-up costs, and no books are printed until they are paid for. Unlike a royalty publisher, the Print on Demand publisher doesn't take any risks. The author takes only a small risk, the reasonable cost to set up the publication.

This is a perfect arrangement for someone who is more interested in writing than in the business part of storing and selling books, collecting money, and sending the books thought the mail to purchasers. The author's only part will be to take his royalty check out of his mailbox and cash it. Some Print on Demand companies make this even easier by offering direct deposit into your bank account.

There are dozens of Print on Demand companies, and the numbers are increasing rapidly. Some companies are professional in their dealings, others are willing to take advantage of a beginning writer, and others are new and disorganized, or don't run their business in a professional manner. This is one reason that it's important to see their completed work, and talk to someone else who has published through them. A reputable POD will be happy to send you a copy of their work if you request it. They should be available by both phone and e-mail, and answer your e-mail questions within twenty-four to forty-eight business hours.

While deciding which Print on Demand Company you wish to use, your first question will be what they charge. Prices range from the low hundreds to over a thousand dollars. You need to find out what is included in the publishing package you purchase. Some of the less expensive packages are bare bones, with nothing added to the package. If you want an ISBN number or your book listed with Internet bookstores, you may have to pay extra. If this is a book intended strictly for your family, with no intent of selling it to anybody else, an inexpensive minimal package is your best choice. If you want photos, a professional cover, editing, or distribution (having your book listed on the Internet and available to order through bookstores), be sure to find out if the POD includes these services, or if there is an extra charge. When you compare prices, be sure you are comparing equal services.

Your next question should be how much royalty you will receive. I've seen royalties ranging from ten percent to a hundred percent. Be sure to find out if the royalty is based on how much the book sells for, or a percentage of the profits after expenses. Fifty percent of profits may become twenty or thirty percent of total sales after the publisher, POD Company, and computer-based sales company (Amazon.com, Barnes & Nobles, Booksamillion etc) are paid. Companies that pay higher royalties often, but not always, have greater up front fees. Check on author discounts when you buy a single book, and when you buy in bulk. Find out if they have special offers when you purchase for a book signing or presentation. Ask if they have any special programs to help you advertise your book, or get it into bookstores.

Getting your POD book into major bookstores ranges from difficult to impossible. Bookstores refuse to buy books that can't be returned, and POD books are sold with a no return policy. Publishing houses print books thousands at a time, which makes the cost of a single book minimal. When books from a standard, or royalty publishing company, don't sell within a certain time frame, bookstores send them back for a refund. However, to save packaging and shipping costs, they don't send the whole book back but only the cover, and they throw away the inside (selling a coverless book is considered theft, and is illegal). Print on Demand books are comparatively expensive since they are published one at a time, and such destruction would be far too costly. POD's are not bought on credit, but must be purchased previous to printing, and are non-refundable, which translates to not being placed in bookstores. Even if a bookstore is willing to place your book, it must be listed with and ordered through a major distributing company such as Ingram or Baker and Taylor. Be sure to ask which distributor the POD Company is using.

Another important thing to look for while deciding which POD to choose is how it handles money. Because the author doesn't collect any money, you are at the mercy of the POD to accurately record sales and pay you. Not all Print on Demand companies are willing to show the author how many sales have been made. Before you sign up with a POD, make sure you've seen a sample of their website where they report sales to you. Talk to someone who has been using this company and ask them if the website is kept up-to-date, and if the information and payments are accurate, and royalty checks are on time. Ask the company when they send out checks. They should give you exact dates, not approximations. Many Print on Demand companies send your royalties only once every three months, which is when Ingram pays them. In addition, few POD companies will pay you on earnings less than twenty-five dollars. They hold your money until they owe you twenty-five dollars or more before sending you a check. Some will directly deposit checks of less than twenty-five dollars into your bank account, but others don't have this service.

Once you've looked at the financial end of publishing, you will want to investigate what services you will be getting for your money. Generally, POD publishers offer several packages and you may add services that aren't included in your package. It's a bit like ordering in a restaurant, you can order a meal, or ala cart.

Most Print on Demand companies will take any book, or have minimal limitations such as no pornography. Some read the book before accepting it, but they are generally looking for minimal quality rather than a bestseller. Since the author has paid the publishing costs, the POD isn't incurring any risk, and makes their living by accepting as many books as possible. Because you pay them for the set-up costs, POD companies make money even if your book never sells. This is why they will be happy to accept your memoirs, written only for your children or family reunion. Some companies offer an option, to have the book published as is, or to have it reviewed. A book that has been reviewed guarantees a minimal quality and, according to the publisher, higher prestige, but this could add hundreds of dollars to your basic set-up cost.

When you examine a book from the company you are considering, check out how it looks inside. You want a book that looks professional. The font (print size) is important. There are some POD companies which use small print to save pages, and lower the publishing cost. I'd rather charge a dollar or two more and have a book that is easy to read and looks professional, than one that is crowded into as few pages as possible. Some POD companies give you a choice of the inside format, but many don't. Some give you a choice relating to the page size your book will be. That has never been important to me, and I let them do whatever they think is best. If you have a preference, be sure you talk about it with the POD before hiring them.

Check the quality of the cover. Some POD companies use cheap paper and low quality print, while others print professional quality books. Make sure you are getting the quality you are paying for. If you have photos you want included, ask about what quality you can expect, and ask to see a book with pictures. Most companies will print a limited number of black and white photos. The cover should be in color, and include a description of the book, a short biography, referred to as a bio, about the author, and a colored photograph of the author, if you wish.

Like all business arrangements, Print on Demand companies will give you a contract to sign. Read it carefully and ask questions. It might be worth your while to have a literary attorney examine the contract and explain it to you. However, POD companies are relatively new and your attorney may be unfamiliar with their contract style. Be sure the payment arrangement is clearly explained. You need to know how much you will be paid, and when. It's also important to have the ability to cancel the contract any time you desire with a minimal notice time. I've heard of agents or royalty publishers purchasing a book which was first published through a POD company. You want to be free to leave your POD whenever you choose, for any reason.

Most Print on Demand companies offer proofreading services. These are recommended, but can more than double the cost of publishing your book. If you can't afford professional proofreading, try to get help from a friend who enjoys reading, and ideally, is a writer himself. It's impossible to objectively proofread your own writing, and a fresh eye is needed to help you catch as many mistakes as possible. However, even with professional proofreading, a few small mistakes are likely to sneak through. Don't fret when you find mistakes after your book has been carefully proofread, and then published—it's rare to find a book without at least a few errors.

Once you send your manuscript to your chosen POD company (most prefer that you send it over the Internet), they will put it in finished format and send these proofs back to you to look over and correct. This isn't the time for a major rewrite, but rather to find any mistakes in the set-up. Check how many corrections your POD company allows, and what they charge for additional corrections.

Some POD companies only publish soft-cover books, while others print hard covers for an extra charge. If having your book in a hardcover format is important to you, then be sure you check to see if your chosen POD does this.

If you don't have an idea for designing the cover, the POD Company will design a cover for you from their standard forms, or will customize it for an extra charge. I design my covers and the POD Company helps me turn my idea into a professional looking cover. I like my covers to be bright and stand out. Most of your sales will be over the Internet, and the first step to making a sale is to have the customer notice your book above all the others.

Most POD companies offer packages to help you promote and sell your book. It's up to you if you decide to do nothing more than put your book on the

Internet and hope it sells, if you make it your full time job to promote your book, or find something between these two extremes that fits your time and interest. As the author, you will probably purchase books to sell or give away yourself. You may want to arrange speeches or book signings to help you sell your book. You may also want to advertise over the Internet. I use my signature— www.FalknerBooks.com—at the bottom of my e-mail to inform people about my books. Since I write nonfiction, I often write to people who have websites with a topic relating to one of my books, and tell them about it. In addition, there are companies that will help you advertise over the Internet and organizations that will allow you to add a link from their website to yours without charge. If your book is well-written, has an interesting cover, and you work to promote it, I guarantee your book will sell, and when you tell people "I'm an author," they will believe it, and so will you.

Web Sites that will give you more information about Print on Demand Publishing.

www.booksandtales.com/pod/index.html
www.angelfire.com/indie/printondemand/PODs.html
www.iUniverse.com
www.Virtualbookworm.com
www.llumina.com
hwww.aventinepress.com
www.actiontales.com

Chapter 14

MY LIFE AS AN AUTHOR

If you ask me what I do, I'll most likely tell you I write. If you ask how I make a living, I'll tell you I'm a mental health counselor, a job I love. No matter if I'm writing a book, counseling, or answering e-mail, I spend much of my day writing.

When I get up in the morning, I turn the computer on to warm up while I'm exercising, showering, getting dressed, and brushing my teeth. I generally read my e-mail, eat breakfast, and then work on a book before leaving for work. Writing isn't something special I do, it's just part of my morning routine. It's also part of my evening routine, and I usually write for two or three hours before going to bed at night. First, I write whatever reports I need to do for my paying job, and then I get into my real writing, my beloved books.

I've always been a late night person, and I enjoy the cool, quiet, late night hours. I try to get to bed before midnight, but it isn't unusual for me to get lost in my writing and find myself nodding at the computer screen around two in the morning. I like to leave the door open for a breeze and listen to the frogs and a surprising variety of wildlife that lives hidden among human habitation. The most common are owls, raccoons, opossums, and an occasional armadillo. I have the luxury of setting my own work hours and rarely work before noon. Working earlier cuts into either my sleeping, or my writing.

Working late at night is only one way I protect my writing time. My friends and family know that I'm not available until I've finished my morning writing. If I miss writing for more than a day or two, I become restless and feel as though something is wrong. If something comes up that limits my morning writing, I am flexible enough to move my writing to later in the day. I don't think I was always this addicted, but writing has been an important part of my life for a long time.

Keep your day job. Until you are earning enough money to live on, consider writing a hobby and something to enjoy, but not an occupation. Very few authors become rich writing. In fact, very few people even make a living writing. Most overnight successes have been writing for ten or more years. I figure my time has come due and any day someone will come knocking at my door offering me a multi-million dollar advance. But until that happens, I'll fit my writing in-between the demands of my paid job, my friends, and my family.

Staying home and writing full time is difficult for most people. When I stayed home writing for a year, I missed the day-to-day interactions I had with other people. Eventually, I needed more stimulation and returned to my full time job, and part time writing career.

I'd like to tell you more, but it's a holiday weekend and my son wants to go out with me. No matter how important writing is, it's even more important to keep a balance in your life. Make sure you set aside time for your health, your friends, and family. Get away from your writing for a while everyday, and spend time with non-writers, people who have their feet firmly on the ground. They will help you keep focused on what, and who, is most important in your life. Taking care of yourself and being available for the important people in your life will strengthen you as a person, and in turn, enrich you as a writer.

Happy writing. I'm looking forward to reading your first book!

0-595-29435-9

Made in the USA
Lexington, KY
29 November 2012